SpringerBriefs in Educational Communications and Technology

Series Editors

J. Michael Spector, University of North Texas, Denton, TX, USA

M. J. Bishop, University System of Maryland, Adelphi, MD, USA

Dirk Ifenthaler, Learning, Design and Technology, University of Mannheim, Mannheim, Baden-Württemberg, Germany

Published in collaboration with the AECT (Association for Educational Communications and Technology), Springer Briefs in Educational Communications and Technology focuses on topics of keen current interest in the broad area of educational information science and technology. Each Brief is intended to provide an introduction to a focused area of educational information science and technology, giving an overview of theories, issues, core concepts and/or key literature in a particular field. A brief could also provide:

- A timely report of state-of-the art analytical techniques and instruments in the field of educational information science and technology,
- A presentation of core concepts,
- An overview of a testing and evaluation method,
- A snapshot of a hot or emerging topic or policy change,
- An in-depth case study,
- A literature review,
- A report/review study of a survey, or
- An elaborated conceptual framework on model pertinent to educational information science and technology. The intended audience for Educational Communications and Technology is researchers, graduate students and professional practitioners working in the general area of educational information science and technology; this includes but is not limited to academics in colleges of education and information studies, educational researchers, instructional designers, media specialists, teachers, technology coordinators and integrators, and training professionals.

Michail Giannakos

Experimental Studies in Learning Technology and Child–Computer Interaction

Michail Giannakos
Department of Computer Science
Norwegian University of Science & Technology
Trondheim, Norway

This book is an open access publication.

ISSN 2196-498X   ISSN 2196-4998   (electronic)
SpringerBriefs in Educational Communications and Technology.
ISBN 978-3-031-14349-6   ISBN 978-3-031-14350-2   (eBook)
https://doi.org/10.1007/978-3-031-14350-2

© Association for Educational Communications and Technology (AECT) 2022
Open Access   This book is licensed under the terms of the Creative Commons Attribution 4.0 International License (http://creativecommons.org/licenses/by/4.0/), which permits use, sharing, adaptation, distribution and reproduction in any medium or format, as long as you give appropriate credit to the original author(s) and the source, provide a link to the Creative Commons license and indicate if changes were made.
The images or other third party material in this book are included in the book's Creative Commons license, unless indicated otherwise in a credit line to the material. If material is not included in the book's Creative Commons license and your intended use is not permitted by statutory regulation or exceeds the permitted use, you will need to obtain permission directly from the copyright holder.
The use of general descriptive names, registered names, trademarks, service marks, etc. in this publication does not imply, even in the absence of a specific statement, that such names are exempt from the relevant protective laws and regulations and therefore free for general use.
The publisher, the authors, and the editors are safe to assume that the advice and information in this book are believed to be true and accurate at the date of publication. Neither the publisher nor the authors or the editors give a warranty, expressed or implied, with respect to the material contained herein or for any errors or omissions that may have been made. The publisher remains neutral with regard to jurisdictional claims in published maps and institutional affiliations.

This Springer imprint is published by the registered company Springer Nature Switzerland AG
The registered company address is: Gewerbestrasse 11, 6330 Cham, Switzerland

In loving memory of my grandfather, Nikitas Koveos (1925-2022), who taught me the value of hard work, respect and kindness.

Prologue

In the turn of the millennium I was making my first steps in the field of child-computer interaction coming from a computer science background and thus with little training in empirical research methods. What was driving my efforts then and what still drives many researchers in the field of child-computer interaction is to create new digital technologies for children, related concepts and interaction paradigms that will render the use of these technologies pleasurable and beneficial for children. Like others in this situation, I soon found myself overwhelmed by the vast literature on methodology, measurements, experiment design, and data analysis, quantitative or qualitative, and still having to make a substantial step to translate methods and practices developed in for social sciences, to address the challenges and choices that I was facing in the field of child-computer interaction.

Many researchers like me have learnt to design their experiments and navigate these choices by trying and learning from failures and successes in their own research and those reported in the growing body of literature on child-computer interaction and interaction design and children. While these fields of inquiry continue to borrow and learn from neighboring disciplines such as human-factors, psychology, health, and the learning sciences, this approach is not the most efficient for starting researchers. The research approaches used have grown substantially over the years to include research through design, the use of analytics, and even artificial intelligence techniques, making the challenges described above even more substantial for researchers making their first steps in this field now. To move beyond trial and error and an eclectic approach to research methods, the field of child-computer interaction needs to develop its own resources and a common ground regarding methodologies, challenges, and best practices for conducting empirical research.

With this book Michalis Giannakos makes an important advance to address this need, with this tutorial introduction for graduate students and researchers. Giannakos is one of the protagonists in research in child-computer interaction and especially its overlap with the field of Educational Technologies. Despite their neighborhood, these fields have different intellectual traditions and adopt diverse research paradigms, so researchers arriving at them from any direction are well served by this introduction to experimental research methods. This book provides a succinct account of the challenges and common approaches for empirical research with children, especially in relation to experimental research.

Next to guiding beginning researchers in an efficient and focused way, the book contributes a valuable point of reference to the evolving multidisciplinary child-computer interaction research community, where individual researchers unfamiliar with experimental methods need them in their own research or in evaluating the research of others.

The illustrates the variety of methods and conflicting world paradigms apply raising the reader's awareness to the typical social settings for experimental studies, the different degrees of engagement of the researcher with the children and their circle (parents, teachers, friend). Later chapters act metaphorically as a gateway with pointers to specialized literature and resources, overviewing the various artifacts that occupy this subfield of inquiry, such as dashboards and avatars. It provides overviews of tools supporting data management and sensemaking of learning analytics, and an overview of practices regarding the analysis of learning data in this field, core concepts like learner-modeling is introduced and different tools to visualize learning, typical measures used in analytics and examples of their application.

Panos Markopoulos

Preface

Many interaction design and learning technology students are introduced to how to design an interface or a service, and how to conduct a study to evaluate it over its indended use. Appropriate methods have been employed extensively over many years to build scientific knowledge and to understand how to design and evaluate technology that supports human needs (e.g., learning, socializing, and well-being). Depending on someone's background and indended training (e.g., computer science, learning sciences, design) the focus can be on the ideation, design, development, evaluation, continuous use, and/or impact. This short book has been written to support the development of those students, and it is tailored to address how technology can support the learning process and how to take account of the uniqueness of the child as an end-user. Therefore, instead of seeing learning as just one domain among others and the child as just one of many end-users, this book uniquely focuses on child-centered and learner-centered perspectives.

During my PhD work in 2009–2013, child-computer interaction (CCI) research had a steady growth stemming primarily from the human-computer interaction (HCI) field (but also from the fields of the learning sciences and design), and the learning technology research landscape was revamping due to the introduction of learning analytics. During the last decade we have seen learning technology and CCI leveraging new opportunities stemming from the inception of new methodologies, technological affordances, and computational analysis techniques (usually connected with the use of data science and AI). The work described in this book is based on advancements in learning technology and CCI research from 2010 onwards. The best practices and indicative examples showcased are either directly connected to my own work, or indirectly to works I have participated and/or supervised.

Books focusing in experimental studies with human-factors in IT-related fields do exist, and several of those books can support someone's training in learning technology and CCI. However, those books are not tailored to address how technology can support human's learning or child's needs. Since there is no approach to interaction design and software development that is best for all types of domains and end-users, a focused approach that takes into account of the uniqueness of the learner and child as end-users is called for.

The book has the following intended audiences:

- Post-graduate level courses (master/PhD) related to educational technology, interaction design, instructional design, and HCI/CCI, which are offered in relevant study programs (e.g., computer science, learning sciences, teachers' education, instructional design)
- Doctoral level self-study in educational technology, interaction design, instructional design, and HCI/CCI, as well as a handbook for the respective summer/winter school or any other intensive course setting.
- Professionals with relevant experience and responsibilities related to design, development, or use of interactive technologies for supporting learning and/or children, as a way to improve their professional activity

Many students have learnt to design and develop a system (e.g., CS graduates) or have been introduced to various technologies to support learning or children's lives (e.g., teacher graduates), but have limited training in conducting a study to evaluate the effectiveness or appropriateness of a certain technology. Relevant courses and materials are often a mix of general material (to HCI or the learning sciences) and presentation/papers of the favorite approaches of the instructor. Thus I believe that this short book can provide a comprehensive introduction to CCI and learning technologies as interdisciplinary fields of research and support students' knowledge on how to evaluate the circumstances that favor (or do not favor) the use of experiments; to make the necessary methodological decisions about the type and features of the experiment; to design the necessary "artifacts" (e.g., prototype systems, interfaces, materials, and procedures); to operationalize and conduct experimental procedures to minimize potential bias; and to report the results of their studies for successful dissemination in top-tier venues (such as journals and conferences).

Trondheim, Norway   Michail Giannakos

Acknowledgments

A large number of people need to be mentioned for their direct or indirect support. First, I would like to thank the collaborators and co-authors of projects and articles that helped in materializing some of the content of this book. The contribution of most of them is also visible in the references of the book; however, many collaborators have contributed in an indirect way.

During the last almost decade at the Norwegian University of Science and Technology (NTNU), I have had the pleasure to collaborate with a number of master's students, doctoral researchers, postdocs, and faculty members, including Hallvard Trætteberg, Monica Divitini, Letizia Jaccheri, Alf Inge Wang, Patrick Mikalef, Ilias Pappas, Sofia Papavlasopoulou, Kshitij Sharma, Katerina Mangaroska, Boban Vesin, Serena Lee-Cultura, Giulia Cosentino, Guttorm Sindre, Jonas Asheim, John Krogstie, Zacharoula Papamitsiou, Trond Aalberg, Jama Noor, Sobah Abbas Petersen, Lukas Cetusic, Marikken Høiseth, Ioannis Leftheriotis, Jakob Westermoen, Martin Lunde, Evan Niforatos, Camilla Tran, Benjamin Fimreite, Andine Luick, Fredrik Monsen, August Solvang, and Aslak Hollund. Moreover, a number of people have also been influential through regular lunch or coffee scientific discourse, including Babak Farschchian, Birgit Krogstie, Yngve Dahl, Patrick Jost, Rune Sætre, Adrian Stoica, Rabail Tahir, Dag Svanæs, Eric Monteiro, Jingyue Li, and Tor Stålhane. I am grateful to my NTNU colleagues, thanks for being such great collaborators and coworkers.

Beyond NTNU, there are also a number of people with whom I have collaborated with during the years among others, Vassilis Kostakos, Peter Brusilovsky, Dragan Gašević, Pierre Dillenbourg, Demetrios Sampson, Niels van Berkel, Panos Markopoulos, Janet Read, Juan Pablo Hourcade, Ole Sejer Iversen, Mutlu Cukurova, Michael Horn, Daniel Spikol, Athanasios Vourvopoulos, Symeon Retalis, Daniele Di Mitri, Xavier Ochoa, and Georgios Yannakakis.

To ensure the quality of this book, I had the fortune of receiving feedback from several people. First, the support of several members from the CCI and the learning technology communities, who provided direct feedback and comments, Panos Markopoulos, Kshitij Sharma, and Sofia Papavlasopoulou. Special thanks to Panos who also accepted to write a foreword for this book. Second, the content behind the book was used as teaching materials for the graduate level "learning technology and analytics" course at NTNU (class 2021–2022). I am very grateful for the feedback and recommendations received from the students of this course.

This book is primarily written to support the students in the Department of Computer Science at NTNU, especially the graduate students participating to our MSc with a specialization on "Interaction Design, Game and Learning Technology." The book would not have been possible without the support from NTNU; the awarded sabbatical allowed me the quality time needed to write up this book. I should also thank the funding bodies of the various projects that contributed to the book; many of the outcomes described in the book have been funded by the Norwegian Research Council, the European Commission, the National Agency for Quality in Education (NOKUT), and the European Research Consortium for Informatics and Mathematics (ERCIM); as well as institutional funding such as the NTNU's Teaching Excellence program (NTNU Toppundervisning) and NTNU's outstanding academic fellowship program (NTNU Stjerneprogrammet). Moreover, I would like to thank NTNU for the financial support for publishing this book as open access, I hope that this will not only make it accessible to NTNU students but also allow students from abroad to benefit. Moreover, I would also like to thank the editors of the Springer Briefs of the Association for Educational Communications and Technology (AECT) for accepting to publish this book and especially Michael Spector for his comments and support though his crystallized intelligence.

Finally I would like to thank my parents and my partner for their daily support and love.

Michail Giannakos

Abstract

Experiments and appropriate experimental methods have been employed extensively over many years to build scientific knowledge and to understand how to design technology to support human needs (e.g., learning, socializing, and well-being). The present book discusses ways in which experiments can be employed in the context of research on learning technology and/or child-computer interaction (CCI). Our intention is to support researchers in these fields to employ experimental studies and increase the quality and rigor of their studies. Interim guidelines and best practices exist in neighboring fields with a long tradition in experimental methods (e.g., the learning sciences, behavioral sciences, and psychology), and many of these practices already apply in CCI and learning technology research. However, with this book we provide a complete and comprehensive description on how to design, implement, and report experiments, with a focus on and examples from CCI and learning technology research. The topics we cover include an introduction to CCI and learning technologies as interdisciplinary fields of research, how to design educational interfaces and visualizations that support your experimental studies, types of experiments and their advantages and disadvantages, methodological decisions in designing and conducting experiments (e.g., devising hypotheses and selecting measures), and reporting your results. We give a brief introduction on how contemporary advances in data science, artificial intelligence, and sensor data have impacted learning technology and CCI research. We also discuss three important issues that a learning technology and CCI researcher needs to be aware of: the importance of the context, ethical considerations, and working with children. The motivation behind and emphasis of this book is helping prospective CCI and learning technology researchers (a) to evaluate the circumstances that favor (or do not favor) the use of experiments, (b) to make the necessary methodological decisions about the type and features of the experiment, (c) to design the necessary "artifacts" (e.g., prototype systems, interfaces, materials, and procedures), (d) to operationalize and conduct experimental procedures to minimize potential bias, and (e) to report the results of their studies for successful dissemination in top-tier venues (such as journals and conferences).

Keywords Experimental studies, Experimental methods, CCI, Learning technology, User studies, Methodological decisions, Reporting, Publishing

Contents

1 **Introduction** 1
　References 5

2 **Learning Technology and Child–Computer Interaction** 7
　2.1　Definitions and Commonalities 7
　2.2　Synergies and Complementarities 11
　References 13

3 **Educational Interface Design and the Role of Artifacts** 15
　3.1　Design of Educational Interfaces 15
　3.2　Artifacts and Treatment Design 20
　References 25

4 **Educational Data, Learning Analytics and Dashboards** 27
　4.1　Educational Data and Learning Analytics 27
　4.2　Learner Modeling 30
　4.3　Educational Dashboards and Visualization 32
　References 35

5 **Common Types of Experimental Designs in CCI and Learning Technology Research** 37
　5.1　Randomized (True) Experiments 40
　5.2　Quasi-Experiments 41
　5.3　Repeated Measures Experiments 41
　5.4　Time Series Experiments 43
　References 45

6 **Data Collection and Analysis in Learning Technology and CCI Research** 47
　6.1　Data Collection 48
　6.2　Data Analysis 60
　References 65

7	**Reporting CCI and Learning Technology Research**		69
	7.1	Introduction (and Motivation)	71
	7.2	Background and Related Work	72
	7.3	Methods	73
		7.3.1 Participants	74
		7.3.2 Setting/Procedure	74
		7.3.3 Data Collection	75
		7.3.4 Research Design	75
		7.3.5 Data Analysis	75
	7.4	Findings (or Results)	76
	7.5	Discussion	78
	7.6	Conclusions and Further Research	79
	References		80
8	**Common Criteria, Pitfalls, and Practices in CCI and Learning Technology Research**		81
	8.1	Common Criteria	81
	8.2	Potential Pitfalls	83
	8.3	Useful Practices	84
	References		87
9	**Developments in Data Science and Artificial Intelligence in Learning Technology and CCI Research**		89
	9.1	Data Science	89
	9.2	Artificial Intelligence	91
	9.3	Sensor Data and Multimodal Learning Analytics	92
	References		94
10	**Issues to Consider as a CCI and Learning Technology Researcher**		97
	10.1	Context in Experimental Studies	97
	10.2	Ethical Considerations	99
	10.3	Working with Children	102
	References		103
11	**Summary and Reflections for Learning Technology and CCI Research**		105
	References		107

About the Author

Michail Giannakos is a professor of interaction design and learning technologies in the Department of Computer Science of the Norwegian University of Science and Technology (NTNU). He is the head of the Learner-Computer Interaction lab (https://lci.idi.ntnu.no/), and his research focuses on the design and study of emerging technologies in online and hybrid education settings and on developing new ways for humans to interact with interactive learning systems.

Giannakos has co-authored more than 200 manuscripts published in prestigious peer-reviewed journals and conferences (including *Computers & Education, Computers in Human Behavior, IEEE Pervasive Computing, IEEE TLT, BIT, BJET, ACM TOCE, ACM IDC, ICLS/CSCL, Interact*).

Giannakos, together with Mike Horn, is the Editor-in-Chief of the *International Journal of Child-Computer Interaction* (Elsevier). He is also in the Editorial Board of *IEEE Transactions on Learning Technology, IEEE Transactions on Education, Behaviour & Information Technology*, and the *International Journal of Information Management*, and has served as a guest editor on highly recognized journals such as *BJET, Computers in Human Behavior, ACM TOCE*, and *IEEE Multimedia*. He has served as an evaluator for the European Commission (EC) and the US-NSF, and he recently co-edited *The Multimodal Learning Analytics Handbook* (Springer) and co-authored a textbook on *Educational Data Analytics for Teachers and School Leaders* (Springer).

Giannakos has worked at several research projects funded by diverse sources like the European Commission, Microsoft Research, The Research Council of Norway (RCN), US-NSF, the German Agency for International Cooperation, and Cheng Endowment. Giannakos is one of the experts in the Norwegian task force (formed by the ministry of education and research) for introducing learning analytics to Norwegian K-12 schools and universities. He is also a recipient of a Marie Curie/ERCIM Fellowship, the Norwegian Young Research Talent Award, and he is one of the outstanding academic fellows of NTNU (2017–2022).

Giannakos usually attends the ACM Interaction Design and Children (IDC) conference (he was a Chair for IDC 2018 and PC-chair for IDC 2022), the ACM conference on Innovation and Technology in Computer Science Education (ITiCSE) (he was a Chair for ITiCSE 2020), and the Learning Analytics and Knowledge (LAK) conference.

Chapter 1
Introduction

Abstract As interdisciplinary research fields, child-computer interaction (CCI) and learning technologies have the advantage of enhancing their methods by borrowing from related fields. They represent a research stream that began by applying theories, methods, and tools from a variety of fields, such as the learning sciences, human-computer interaction, design, and the social sciences. Experiments and appropriate experimental methods have been employed extensively over many years to build scientific knowledge and to understand how to design technology to support human needs (e.g., learning, socializing, and wellbeing). This chapter discusses how experiments and experimental studies can be employed in the context of research on learning technology and/or CCI.

Keywords Learning technology · Child-computer interaction · Experimental research · Experimental studies

Scientific research follows an iterative process of observation, rationalization, and validation (Bhattacherjee, 2012). As the name suggests, during an observation, we observe (experience/sense) the phenomenon (e.g., event, behavior, or interaction) of interest, and we form an initial research question (RQ). In many cases, the initial question is anecdotal (e.g., you noticed that students who use dashboards complete more assignments, or the ones participating to more classroom quizzes have better mid-term or final grades), but it can also be based on some data (e.g., you see that the scores of students who complete tasks in the labs are higher than those of students who complete tasks in the classroom). In the rationalization phase, we try to understand a phenomenon by systematically connecting what we have observed, and this might lead to the formation or concretization of a theory or scientific inquiry (e.g., research hypotheses). Finally, the validation phase allows us to test potential research hypotheses and/or theories using an appropriate research design (e.g., data collection and analysis).

The research process should be based on the principles of design research with a very intensive collaboration between practitioners and researchers. The ultimate goal is to build strong connection between research and practice. An emphasis should be placed on the iterative nature of the research process that does not just "test" a technology or a process, but refines the technology or process while also producing new knowledge (e.g., best practices, design principles) that can support future research and development. Closely situating your work in real-world settings and collaborating with stakeholders, allow you to both clearly identify the problem that you seek to solve, and deploy and evaluate our research in their intended environments. Therefore, the proposed iterative process of observation, rationalization, and validation (Fig. 1.1), should be employed in a way to leverage collaboration among researchers and practitioners in real-world settings and lead to contextually-sensitive knowledge, design principles and theories.

The research that is put into practice varies in type. For instance, the researcher can conduct further observations to rationalize the observations already made (something we used to call inductive research) or test the theory or scientific inquiry of interest (something we used to call deductive research). The selection of the type of research depends on the researcher's standpoint on the nature of knowledge (epistemology) and reality (ontology), which is shaped by the disciplinary areas the researcher belongs to. Given their interdisciplinary nature, the fields of child–computer interaction (CCI) and learning technology follow both the inductive and the deductive research traditions. Although parts of this book can apply to both types of research, its focus is more on deductive research and how this can be functionalized through experimental studies.

Experimental research has been used extensively as one of the primary methodologies for a wide range of disciplines, from chemistry to physics to psychology to human–computer interaction (HCI) to the learning sciences (LS). The inherent

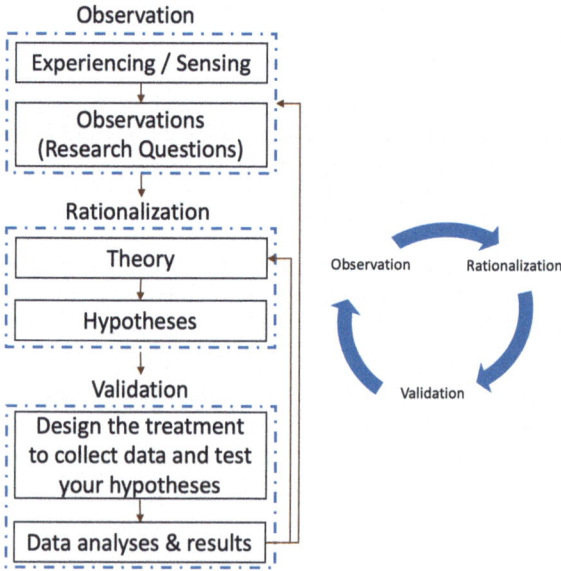

Fig. 1.1 The iterative process of observation, rationalization, and validation

1 Introduction

connections between CCI and learning technology, on the one hand, and HCI and LS, on the other hand, as well as the strong links of all these disciplines to the behavioral sciences, have resulted in the use of experimental studies as one of the predominant modes of research. Experimental studies are often considered to be the "gold standard" (most rigorous) of research designs (Christensen et al., 2011), and from the early 1900s onward, experimental research methods received strong impetus from behavioral research and psychology. The goal of experimental research is to show how the manipulation of a variable of interest (e.g., the resolution of a video lecture) has a direct *causal influence* on another variable of interest (e.g., students' perception of fractions). For instance, we can consider the following research question: "How does the visualization of students' learning scores via a dashboard affect their future learning performance?"

To conceptualize the RQ, the researcher investigates the effect of the experimental/independent variable on the dependent/outcome variable through an induced "treatment" (a procedure that holds all conditions constant except the independent/experimental variable). Therefore, any potential significant difference identified when comparing the group with the induced experimental treatment (the experimental group) to the group without the treatment (the control group) is assumed to have been caused by the independent variable (see Fig. 1.2 for a graphical representation.) Such an experiment ensures high internal validity (the degree to which the design of the experiment controls for extraneous factors). Therefore, in contrast to other types of research, such as descriptive, correlational, survey, and ethnographic studies, experiments create conditions where the outcome can be confidently attributed to the independent variable rather than to other factors. Simply put, an experiment is "a study in which an intervention is deliberately introduced to observe its effects" (Shadish et al., 2002, p. 12).

Experiments are not always easy to define, as they depend on the domain, the RQs, and even the scientist (Cairns et al., 2016). They rely heavily on craft, skill, and experience, and they put tests into practice to trial ideas. In the case of CCI and learning technology, those trials are employed to evaluate existing or new

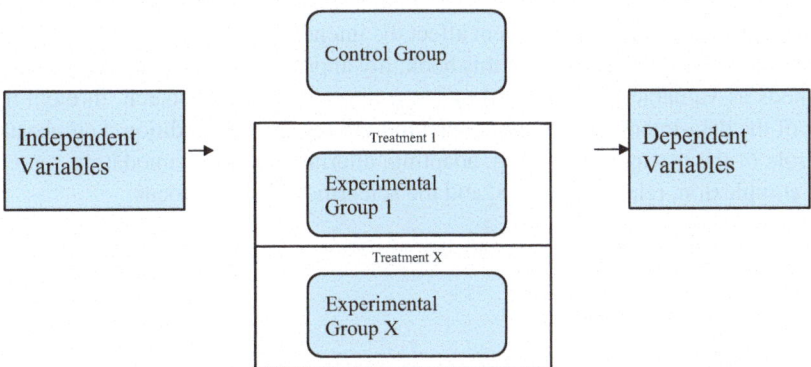

Fig. 1.2 Typical representation of an experiment

technologies and interfaces, establish guidelines, and understand how learners/children use technology. The main strength of the experimental paradigm derives from its high internal validity, which allows experimentation to be viewed as an "acceptable" research practice (Hannafin, 1986). Experimental research gives less emphasis to external validity, which concerns the degree to which the results of a study can be generalized to other situations, particularly realistic ones, a focus that is at the center of other research designs and approaches that are commonly employed in CCI and learning technologies (e.g., Barab & Squire, 2004).

As interdisciplinary research fields, CCI and learning technologies have the advantage of enhancing their methods by borrowing from related fields. They represent a research stream that began by applying theories, methods, and tools from a variety of fields, such as LS, HCI, design, and the social sciences. It is not difficult to see the nature and benefits of interdisciplinarity in CCI and learning technologies that results from the integration of qualities from different fields (e.g., user/learner-centeredness, internal validity, external validity, and accounting for context) and allowing researchers to leverage and combine a wide range of methods, theories, and tools.

The purpose of this book is not to promote or criticize experimental methods, but rather to provide insights for their effective use in CCI and learning technology research. It is important to highlight the importance of "method pluralism" and "letting method be the servant" (Firebaugh, 2018). As in work on experimental methods in human-factor IT-related fields that has criticized "the man of one method or one instrument" (e.g., Hornbæk, 2013; Gergle & Tan, 2014), we want to emphasize the risks of adopting a method-oriented research practice rather than a problem-oriented one. Method-oriented practice is likely to drive researchers to conduct experiments that force-fit the data (Ross & Morrison, 2013) or to dissuade them from conducting experiments when needed, instead relying on methods that center on the experience of the researcher or lead to results that cannot be replicated. As Platt (1964, p. 351) stated, "the method-oriented man is shackled; the problem-oriented man is at least reaching freely toward what is most important."

Experimental studies allow us to isolate which components (e.g., functionalities or affordances) of the technology, the medium, the end-user (e.g., the learner, teacher, or child) or the environment affect the intended goal (e.g., learning or social interaction) and in what ways. In this book, my approach is to present experimental methods as valuable tools for CCI and learning technology research, through the lens of the data-intensive nature of contemporary research. In addition, I emphasize the role of the researcher in using, adapting, altering, and accommodating contextual complexion, relevant theories, and the scientific inquiry of focus.

References

Barab, S., & Squire, K. (2004). Design-based research: Putting a stake in the ground. *The Journal of the Learning Sciences, 13*(1), 1–14.

Bhattacherjee, A. (2012). *Social science research: Principles, methods, and practices*. Global Text Project.

Cairns, P., Soegaard, M., & Dam, R. F. (2016). Experimental methods in human-computer interaction. In M. Soedergaard & R. Dam (Eds.), *Encyclopedia of human-computer interaction* (2nd ed.). Interaction Design Foundation.

Christensen, L. B., Johnson, B., Turner, L. A., & Christensen, L. B. (2011). *Research methods, design, and analysis*. University of South Alabama.

Firebaugh, G. (2018). *Seven rules for social research*. Princeton University Press.

Gergle, D., & Tan, D. S. (2014). Experimental research in HCI. In *Ways of knowing in HCI* (pp. 191–227). Springer.

Hannafin, M. J. (1986). Ile status and future of research in instructional design and technology. *Journal of Instructional Development, 8*, 24–30.

Hornbæk, K. (2013). Some whys and hows of experiments in human–computer interaction. *Foundations and Trends in Human-Computer Interaction, 5*(4), 299–373.

Platt, J. (1964). Strong inference. *Science, 146*(3642), 347–353.

Ross, S. M., & Morrison, G. R. (2013). Experimental research methods. In J. M. Spector, M. D. Merrill, J. Elen, & M. J. Bishop (Eds.), *Handbook of research on educational communications and technology* (pp. 1007–1029). Routledge.

Shadish, W. R., Cook, T. D., & Campbell, D. T. (2002). *Experimental and quasi-experimental designs for generalized causal inference*. Houghton Miffl in.

Open Access This chapter is licensed under the terms of the Creative Commons Attribution 4.0 International License (http://creativecommons.org/licenses/by/4.0/), which permits use, sharing, adaptation, distribution and reproduction in any medium or format, as long as you give appropriate credit to the original author(s) and the source, provide a link to the Creative Commons license and indicate if changes were made.

The images or other third party material in this chapter are included in the chapter's Creative Commons license, unless indicated otherwise in a credit line to the material. If material is not included in the chapter's Creative Commons license and your intended use is not permitted by statutory regulation or exceeds the permitted use, you will need to obtain permission directly from the copyright holder.

Chapter 2
Learning Technology and Child–Computer Interaction

Abstract Learning technology research focuses on the design, development, and/or use of technologies that support learning, whereas CCI research focuses on the design, development, and/or use of technologies that support children's lives (with a heavy emphasis on learning). Therefore, learning technology and CCI research can be described as research that focuses on the design, development, and/or use of technologies that support learning and/or children's lives. In this chapter, we provide an introduction to CCI and learning technologies as interdisciplinary fields of research, provide good working definitions and discuss their commonalities, synergies, and complementarities.

Keywords Learning technology · Child–computer interaction · Definitions · Research fields

2.1 Definitions and Commonalities

One valid question someone might ask is why this short book focuses on learning technology and CCI. Why not just use some of the previously published books or papers in experimental methods and studies in human-factors IT-related fields (e.g., Hornbæk, 2013; Gergle & Tan, 2014; Ross & Morrison, 2013)? After all, learning technology is closely related to the learning and education sciences, and CCI is closely related to interaction design and HCI. What are the commonalities of learning technology and CCI that require a shared technical note? Do we have enough commonalities to justify a book on the subject?

The truth is that books on experimental methods from neighboring research communities (e.g., the learning sciences and the social sciences), and especially those from human-factors IT-related fields (e.g., HCI and information systems), can indeed be used to support researchers in learning technology and CCI. However, those books are not tailored to address how technology can support the learning process or to take account of the uniqueness of the child as an end-user. Instead, they see learning as just one process among others and the child as just one of many end-users. Therefore, this book aims to cover CCI and learning technology more comprehensively than books that focus on HCI, LS, or software engineering, with a unique focus on child-centered and learner-centered perspectives.

Another interesting question concerns whether CCI and learning technology (and the respective child-centered and learner-centered perspectives) can go together. First of all, let us consider how the main publication venues, organizations, and societies of these two fields see themselves, their commonalities, and their differences.

In terms of learning technology, *Computers & Education* journal[1] (the top-ranked educational technology journal according to Google metrics[2]) welcomes research on "knowledge and understanding of ways in which digital technology can enhance education" and "on the pedagogical uses of digital technology, where the focus is broad enough to be of interest to a wider education community." Another reputable but more technical journal, *IEEE Transactions in Learning Technology*,[3] welcomes research on "advances in learning technologies and their applications, including but not limited to: online learning systems; intelligent tutors; educational games; simulation systems for education and training; collaborative learning tools; learning with mobile devices; wearable devices and interfaces for learning ..." The Association for Educational Communications and Technology (AECT) is the oldest professional association for instructional designers and an academic and professional association that promotes educational uses of technology. The AECT defines educational technology as "the study and ethical practice of facilitating learning and improving performance by creating, using and managing appropriate technological processes and resources" (Richey, 2008, p. 24). Another reputable scholar who has served as AECT president and is editor emeritus of the Educational Technology Research & Development (ETR&D), Spector (2015, p. 10), describes educational technology as the "application of knowledge for the purpose of improving learning, instruction and/or performance." By looking closely at the definitions of these leading journals, scholars, and the AECT, we see that the focus is on the design, development, and use of learning technology, with some venues focusing on the use and others on the design/development. For example, we regularly see Computer Science departments focusing on design and development, whereas education/learning sciences departments tend to focus on use (without this being an absolute rule). In reality, however, these different aspects need to be studied jointly and iteratively.

The initiation of CCI as a field of research stems from the 1960s (Giannakos et al., 2020a, b), when pioneering researchers such as Seymour Papert, Edith Ackermann, Marvin Minsky, and Alan Kay explored the design of computer systems for children. In 2002 the research community established the International Conference on Interaction Design and Children (IDC), which is an annual venue for

---

[1] Computers & Education: https://www.journals.elsevier.com/computers-and-education
[2] Google Scholar metrics, educational technology sub-field: https://scholar.google.com/citations?view_op=top_venues&hl=en&vq=eng_educationaltechnology
[3] IEEE Transactions in Learning Technology: https://ieee-edusociety.org/publication/ieee-tlt

2.1 Definitions and Commonalities

research on "the latest research findings, innovative methodologies and new technologies in the areas of inclusive child-centered design, learning and interaction." The *International Journal of Child–Computer Interaction* (IJCCI), which is the only journal focusing explicitly on CCI, welcomes research on knowledge concerning "the phenomena surrounding the interaction between children and computational and communication technologies" (Giannakos et al., 2020a, b, p. 1).

Therefore, it is safe to say that learning technology research focuses on the design, development, and/or use of technologies that support learning, whereas CCI research focuses on the design, development, and/or use of technologies that support children's lives (with a heavy emphasis on learning). If we try to unfold the scope of those two communities, we realize that there are two pillars: the focus area and the developmental stage/age of the end-user. The focus area of learning technology (e.g., learning, teaching, competence development, assessment, and cognition) is a subgroup of CCI, which covers all the focus areas of learning technology, plus others such as sociability, healthcare, and play. The developmental stage/age of the end-user in CCI (from toddlerhood to adolescence) is a subgroup of learning technology, which covers all the end-user groups of CCI, including university students, lifelong learners, and other adult learners. Based on these considerations, learning technology and CCI research can be described as research that focuses on the design, development, and/or use of technologies that support learning and/or children's lives. To clarify the commonalities and differences between learning technology and CCI, we have made a Venn diagram (Fig. 2.1).

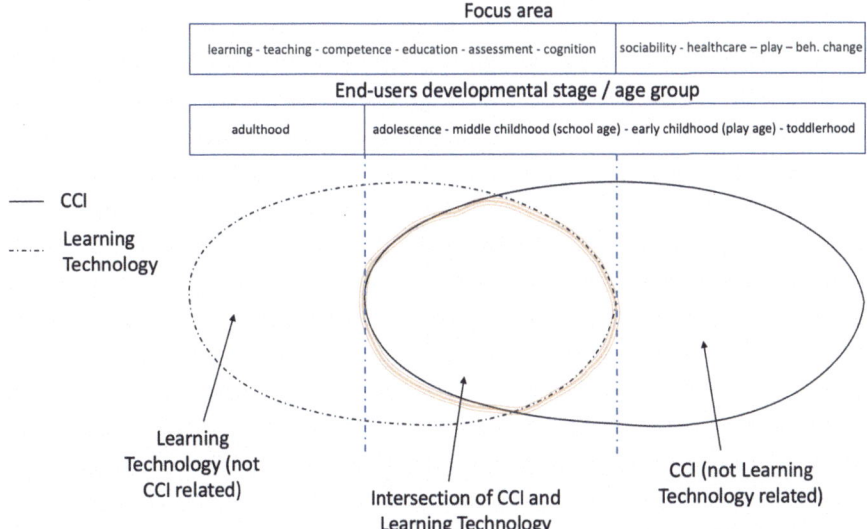

Fig. 2.1 Venn diagram depicting the relationship between CCI and learning technology. (Note: The size of the diagram and the various spaces and sets does not correspond to the amount of research in each field)

Besides the obvious differences stemming from the difference in focus (in learning technology, the user as a learner; in CCI, the user as a child), we see a substantial overlap in the research methods employed and the amount of research that is suitable for both venues. For instance, research in learning technology in K-12 schools or kindergarten and preschool settings is welcomed in CCI research communities and venues. Similarly, research in CCI that focuses on computing/programming education, game-based learning, and constructionism/making in childhood is welcomed in learning technology research communities and venues. A recent analysis of the research themes that have been published in the main CCI venues (i.e., the IDC and *IJCCI*), makes evident the inherent connection between CCI and learning technology (Giannakos et al., 2020b). Therefore, the methodological similarities, substantial overlaps between the research communities, and common thematic areas justify a book that considers CCI and learning technology together. Figure 2.2 shows the volumes and relationships of CCI themes (based on the keywords of published papers); the central role of learning technology (e.g., education as a central theme) is clear.

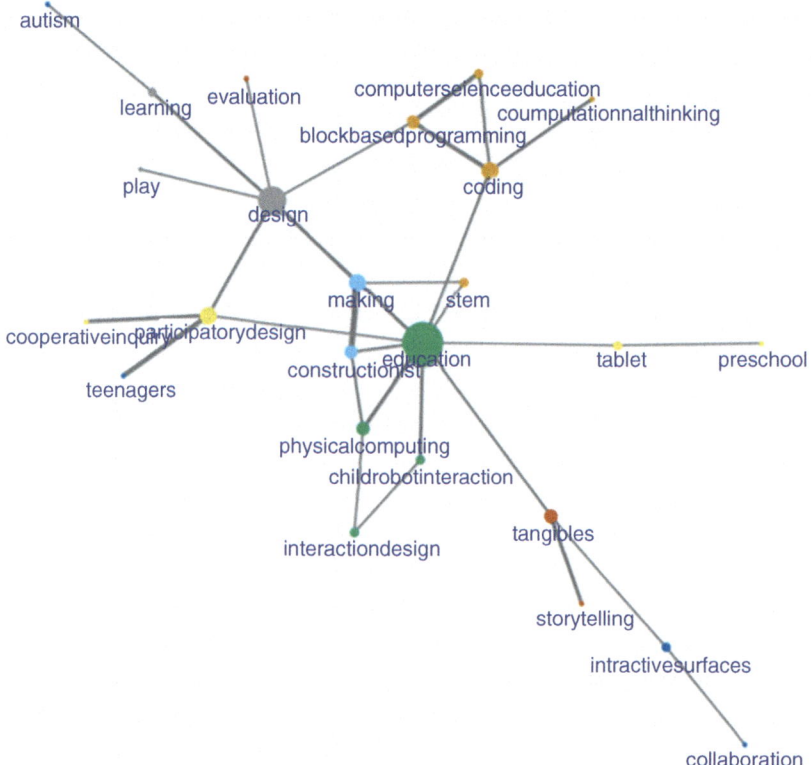

Fig. 2.2 Network map of the keywords of articles published in the two main CCI venues (IDC and IJCCI), 2013–2018. (from Giannakos et al., 2020b; licensed under CC BY-ND 4.0)

2.2 Synergies and Complementarities

As described above, there are various similarities between CCI and learning technology research, and this is why it makes sense to describe the implementation of their experimental studies together. At the same time, there are differences that prospective researchers should take into consideration. The main difference is that one adopts a child-centered perspective and the other a learner-centered perspective. Although these perspectives are not mutually exclusive, it is not always possible or desirable to maintain both (e.g., when conducting learning-at-scale studies in learning technology). The two perspectives also affect the role and participation of the end-user in research and experimentation. The learner (as a user) demonstrates a higher degree of "autonomy" in the experimentation, while the child (as a user) requires significantly more contextual interpretation of the results and investigation to be carried out jointly with their support sphere (i.e., learning facilitators, such as teachers, parents, and therapists).

These differences result in differences in the methods employed and how they are implemented. For example, it is very common in learning technology studies to collect learner-generated data, develop learners' trajectories, and/or explore that data in different ways. This has led learning technology research to focus on the various analytics produced and to explore the role of the various technological processes and resources in supporting learning. A consequence of this paradigm shift (some might say acute need or development in the field) is the "conception" of learning analytics (Siemens, 2013), defined as "the measurement, collection, analysis and reporting of data about learners and their contexts, for purposes of understanding and optimizing learning and the environments in which it occurs" (LAK, 2011). Although child-produced analytics are also used in CCI research, this development has affected CCI to a lesser extent, since the growth of learning analytics stems from the increase in online learning that has taken place during the last decade, particularly in post K-12 settings (e.g., higher education and learning in the workplace).

In CCI, however, children's roles and participation in experimentation has been studied extensively (Markopoulos et al., 2021). Children's roles in the design and evaluation of technology vary according to the maturity of technology prototypes (e.g., low to high fidelity), the expected end-user of the products (e.g., an auxiliary user, or children as primary or secondary users), and the children's ages and abilities (Giannakos et al., 2020a, b). These roles were initially described using three dimensions: the relationship to adults, the relationship to technology, and the goals of the inquiry. Four initial roles for children in the design process have been defined: users, testers, informants, and design partners (Druin, 2002). This distinction between roles has prevailed in CCI research with further efforts to engage children even more intensively in the design process (Iversen et al., 2017). Therefore, methodological approaches have been designed that embrace the fact that children are central participants in experimentation and not just users of the technology (e.g., Frauenberger et al., 2015). Another particularity of CCI research is that in many cases it is neither practical nor possible to collect data directly from the child (the end-user). Therefore, CCI research is often supported by proxy data collections and experiments that include data collection from the children's support sphere (e.g., surveys or interactions with teachers or parents). This might also need researchers' participation during the intervention to obtain insights that cannot be captured via interactions and that teachers or parents have difficulties in "sensing."

In order to clarify potential differences in the approaches employed, Fig. 2.3 gives an overview of three approaches, each with an example and some potential advantages and disadvantages. The first approach is typical for studies that investigate how the child or the learner can autonomously use a technology, this approach is also appropriate for learning-at-scale studies (e.g., a large MOOC or LMS-based intervention); the second approach is used with technologies that are designed for the learner/child and someone from their support sphere as joint primary users (e.g., an intervention to provide technology to support classroom teachers or parents); the third is commonly found when technologies require user insights in the early phases of the design (e.g., an intervention to capture the requirements or define the nature of the services, rather than specific implementation details).

Before concluding this section, we want to emphasize that there is no "good" or" bad" approach here. The aforementioned approaches have been developed and used to meet different objectives and needs. Therefore, when someone asks which approach to use, the answer is that it depends on the purpose and context. Consider the nature of CCI research and the challenges it involves; for example, primary

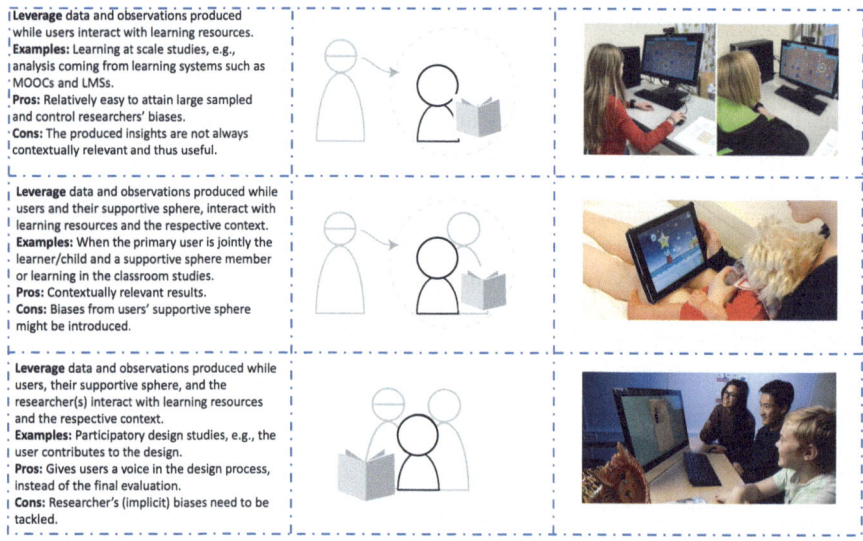

Fig. 2.3 Three different approaches employed in CCI and learning technology research: (1) autonomously use a technology; (2) technologies that are designed for the learner/child and someone from their support sphere as joint primary users; and (3) technologies require user insights and participation in the early phases of the design

school children have not yet fully developed some skills (including language and reading abilities and abstract thinking), and their thinking processes are based on mental representations that relate to concrete events, objects, and experiences. Under those circumstances, it is natural that we should see a number of research endeavors that focus on methods that are participatory and contextually rich. On the other hand, with the increasing interest in "autonomous," "context-independent," and "at-scale" learning technologies (e.g., MOOCs and LMSs), it is also natural to see research endeavors that focus on producing large amounts of educational data to account for different contexts. Of course, synergies between the different approaches do exist, and all the aforementioned approaches are relevant for both CCI and learning technology research.

Advancing our understanding and the appropriate approaches and methodological processes in relation to children's and learners' roles and participation in research, as well as furthering their engagement in the design process, is at the top of both the CCI and the learning technology research agendas (e.g., Giannakos et al., 2020a, b; DiSalvo et al., 2017). Therefore, continuing to develop and advance synergies on the methodological front between CCI and learning technology is a way to cross-fertilize and accelerate progress.

References

DiSalvo, B., Yip, J., Bonsignore, E., & Carl, D. (2017). *Participatory design for learning* (pp. 3–6). Routledge.
Druin, A. (2002). The role of children in the design of new technology. *Behaviour and Information Technology, 21*(1), 1–25.
Frauenberger, C., Good, J., Fitzpatrick, G., & Iversen, O. S. J. (2015). In pursuit of rigour and accountability in participatory design. *International Journal of Human Computer Studies, 74*, 93–106.
Gergle, D., & Tan, D. S. (2014). Experimental research in HCI. In *Ways of knowing in HCI* (pp. 191–227). Springer.
Giannakos, M. N., Horn, M. S., Read, J. C., & Markopoulos, P. (2020a). Movement forward: The continued growth of child-computer interaction research. *International Journal of Child-Computer Interaction, 26*. https://doi.org/10.1016/j.ijcci.2020.100204
Giannakos, M., Papamitsiou, Z., Markopoulos, P., Read, J., & Hourcade, J. P. (2020b). Mapping child–computer interaction research through co-word analysis. *International Journal of Child-Computer Interaction, 23*, 100165.
Hornbæk, K. (2013). Some whys and hows of experiments in human–computer interaction. *Foundations and Trends in Human-Computer Interaction, 5*(4), 299–373.
Iversen, O. S., Smith, R. C., & Dindler, C. (2017). Child as protagonist: Expanding the role of children in participatory design. In *Proceedings of the 2017 conference on interaction design and children* (pp. 27–37).
LAK. (2011). *Proceedings of the 1st international conference on learning analytics and knowledge*. Association for Computing Machinery.
Markopoulos, P., Read, J., & Giannakos, M. (2021). Design of digital technologies for children. In G. Salvendy & W. Karwowski (Eds.), *Handbook of human factors and ergonomics* (5th ed.). Wiley.

Richey, R. C., Silber, K. H., & Ely, D. P. (2008). Reflections on the 2008 AECT definitions of the field. *TechTrends, 52*(1), 24–25.
Ross, S. M., & Morrison, G. R. (2013). Experimental research methods. In *Handbook of research on educational communications and technology* (pp. 1007–1029). Routledge.
Siemens, G. (2013). Learning analytics: The emergence of a discipline. *American Behavioral Scientist, 57*(10), 1380–1400.
Spector, J. M. (2015). *Foundations of educational technology: Integrative approaches and interdisciplinary perspectives*. Routledge.

Open Access This chapter is licensed under the terms of the Creative Commons Attribution 4.0 International License (http://creativecommons.org/licenses/by/4.0/), which permits use, sharing, adaptation, distribution and reproduction in any medium or format, as long as you give appropriate credit to the original author(s) and the source, provide a link to the Creative Commons license and indicate if changes were made.

The images or other third party material in this chapter are included in the chapter's Creative Commons license, unless indicated otherwise in a credit line to the material. If material is not included in the chapter's Creative Commons license and your intended use is not permitted by statutory regulation or exceeds the permitted use, you will need to obtain permission directly from the copyright holder.

Chapter 3
Educational Interface Design and the Role of Artifacts

Abstract User interfaces (UI) are an inherent part of any technology with human end-users. The design of the UI depends heavily on the intended end-user and is therefore extremely important for research in both learning technology (where the learner is the end-user) and CCI (where the child is the end-user). Another important concept of learning technology and CCI research (and also in neighboring fields) is that of "artifact". Artifacts correspond to novel designs (which may be prototype systems, interfaces, materials, or procedures) that have a certain set of qualities or components (such as functionalities and affordances) and that allow us to experiment (e.g., to isolate and test certain components). This chapter describes how researchers can design educational interfaces, visualizations, and other artifacts to support their experiments and enhance learners' and children's experience with technology.

Keywords Learning technology · Educational interfaces · Artifacts · Artefacts · Interaction design

3.1 Design of Educational Interfaces

User interfaces are an inherent part of any technology with human end-users. The role of an interface is to facilitate efficient communication and information exchange between the machine (the technology) and the user (the human). User interfaces (UIs) rely on what we call "interface metaphors," sets of visuals, actions, and procedures incorporated into the UI that exploit specific knowledge that users already have of other domains, such as their homes and working environments. The use of proper interface metaphors allows users to predict the functionalities of each element of the interface (metaphor), resulting in more intuitive use of the interface and more predictable system behavior. Confusion is avoided, as there is no need for explanations of the various elements of the UI, and users are aware of the impact that their actions will have on the system. A time-tested example is the "desktop" metaphor, which portrays the operating system as similar to objects, tasks, and behaviors found in physical office environments (Neale & Carroll, 1997).

The appropriate selection and application of UI metaphors make systems easy to use, and so we need to understand how metaphors are perceived by our targeted end-users. Good understanding will allow us to incorporate metaphors efficiently into our UIs. Below, we provide some commonly used metaphors that allow UI designers to develop intuitive interfaces. As technology advances and different applications are developed (including new ways of working, living, learning, and communicating), new metaphors need to be established to increase the usability of those applications. The examples show the centrality of metaphor to UI and the importance of drawing on real-world analogies (Table 3.1).

The selection of metaphors and the design of the UI depend heavily on the intended end-user and are therefore extremely important for research in both learning technology (where the learner is the end-user) and CCI (where the child is the end-user). For example, a straightforward note-making metaphor (e.g., for presenting new information) might be good for a technology that targets teachers but less effective for a technology that targets doctors (where a Post-it metaphor might work better). The same applies to all user groups, although learners and children are particularly interesting end-users. Learning is not always an easy process. It is associated with many aspects of interaction and cognition (including difficult mental operations and cognitive friction), and these differ across the different developmental phases of a child. For instance, for very young children, even time-tested metaphors such as "desktop" can fail to convey the intended information. Therefore, it is important to work closely with the end-user to develop an appropriate set of visuals, actions, and procedures that can be incorporated into the UI to achieve the intended objectives (see for example, Fig. 3.1, Asheim, 2012; Høiseth et al., 2013). Moreover, learning takes place in and across diverse contexts (e.g., online or in classrooms, labs, and maker spaces), and the content area (e.g., math, language, or art) plays an important role in the mental models generated by the user during learning and the ways in which those models need to be taken into consideration to facilitate learning.

The main focus of metaphors is ease-of-use, usability, and utility for representing a system's functionality (Kuhn & Blumenthal, 1996). However, the capacity of UI

Table 3.1 Some commonly used UI metaphors

Context	Target domain	Source domain	Knowledge used
Information structures	Browsing and searching	Book/dictionary	Pages, bookmarks, tabs, indexes
	Organizing documents	Piles	Physical piles of papers
Group work	Collaborative work spaces	Shared slides/documents	Flip-charts, whiteboard
	Online meeting/conferencing	Phone and video calls	Phone, TV
Virtual reality	Navigating	Flying hand/arrow graphics	Following arrows in the physical and spatial world

3.1 Design of Educational Interfaces

Fig. 3.1 Examples of how to achieve objectives by using familiar and repetitive elements (adopted from: Asheim, 2012; Høiseth et al., 2013, with permission by Asheim and Høiseth)

metaphors to facilitate learning has been historically recognized and valued by both the learning technology and the HCI communities (e.g., see Carroll & Mack, 1985; Neale & Carroll, 1997). Metaphors facilitate learning by leveraging existing mental models or previously learned information and applying them to new contexts (Bruner, 1960). Learning is accelerated when metaphors are used, because they draw on existing knowledge bases to reason about new problems (Streitz, 1988).

Contemporary research and practice recognize the importance of iteration and end-user participation during the UI design (e.g., DiSalvo et al., 2017). Processes from HCI, such as rapid prototyping and low-fidelity paper prototyping (Wilson & Rosenberg, 1988), are commonly used in educational UI. Those practices are advantageous because of their simplicity, low cost (no need for many working hours or materials/tools), and the ease of obtaining early feedback from the end-user. They also adopt the main steps of established instructional system models, such as ADDIE (analysis, design, development, implementation, and evaluation) (Branch, 2009), which allows the necessary steps to unfold iteratively. The powerful progression from a low-fidelity, pen-and-paper prototype to a working system is shown in Fig. 3.2 through two examples, one on the development of a UI for a multi-touch gamified quiz system that supports learning in museums (Noor, 2016), and one on the development of a UI for a self-assessment technology that supports online learning (Westermoen & Lunde, 2020). As the figure shows, the initial low-fidelity ideation is created using only pen and paper. The sketches are very basic, but they also useful for determining how the user will interact with the interface; because the sketches in this phase of the design are low-fidelity, it is easy and "cheap" to change them. After the first iteration, some of the features are developed and tested with a few end-users, but even then it remains easy to test the basic functionalities and accommodate the results from the testing (e.g., in terms of metaphors used, information visualized, and actual functionalities). As the fidelity of the interface increases and more interactive functionalities (and the respective wireframes) are incorporated, it becomes more difficult and costly to accommodate structural

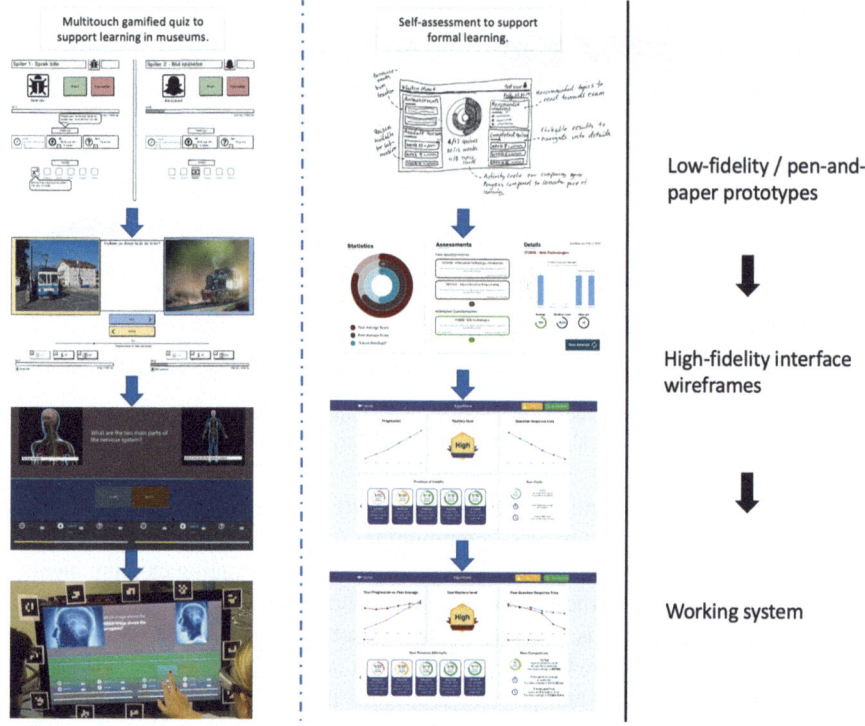

Fig. 3.2 The process from low-fidelity pen-and-paper prototype to a working system. Left: The development of a UI for a multitouch gamified quiz system that supports learning in museums. (From Sharma et al., 2020; licensed under CC BY-ND 4.0). Right: The development of a UI for self-assessment technology that supports online learning. (From Westermoen & Lunde, 2020, with permission by Westermoen and Lunde)

changes. In the final stages of the process, we have a working system that can be tested through experimentation.

Within the progression from low fidelity to high fidelity and ultimately the complete UI, the designer needs to make progress in the development of the navigation thread. The storyboarding/navigation thread will cover all the possible use cases and scenarios and the interconnections within the wireframes. Figure 3.3 shows the storyboarding of a self-assessment UI (adapted from Westermoen & Lunde, 2020). During the design of the educational UI, the designer needs to keep in mind who the intended end-users are (e.g., children, other learners); what their characteristics are (age, background knowledge); the expected objectives (learning goals, competence development); the different types of constraints (learning constraints, technological constraints, teachers' competence); the delivery options and expected role of the technology; and its pedagogical underpinning. In addition to answering these very important questions, the UI designer needs to be able to gather information from end-users and test their ideas.

3.1 Design of Educational Interfaces

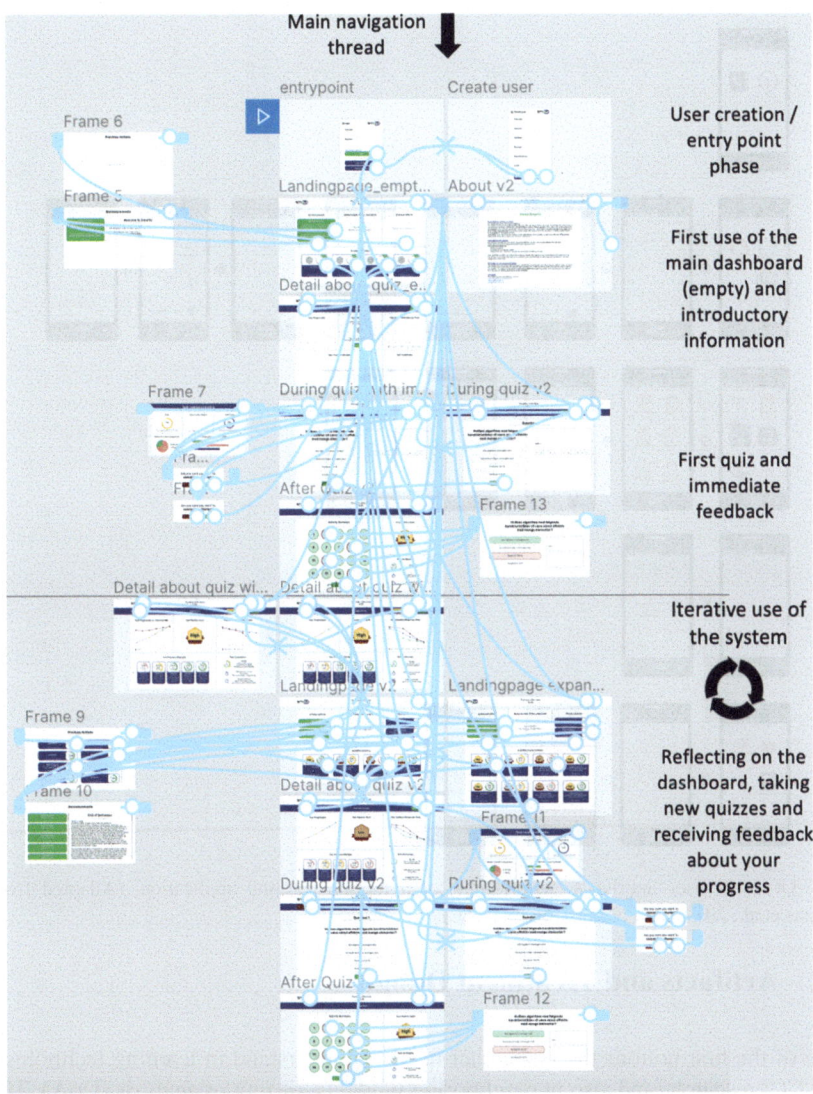

Fig. 3.3 Storyboarding of a self-assessment UI. (Adapted from Westermoen & Lunde, 2020; with permission by Westermoen and Lunde)

As a result of the iterative design process and storyboarding, a collection of wireframes representing each possible view a user might encounter is created. The final UIs need to consider the context of use and provide the necessary guidelines for the implementation of the application. Figure 3.4 shows an example set of UIs in the context of mobile learning in higher education. (More information about this example can be found in Pappas et al., 2017 and Cetusic, 2017)

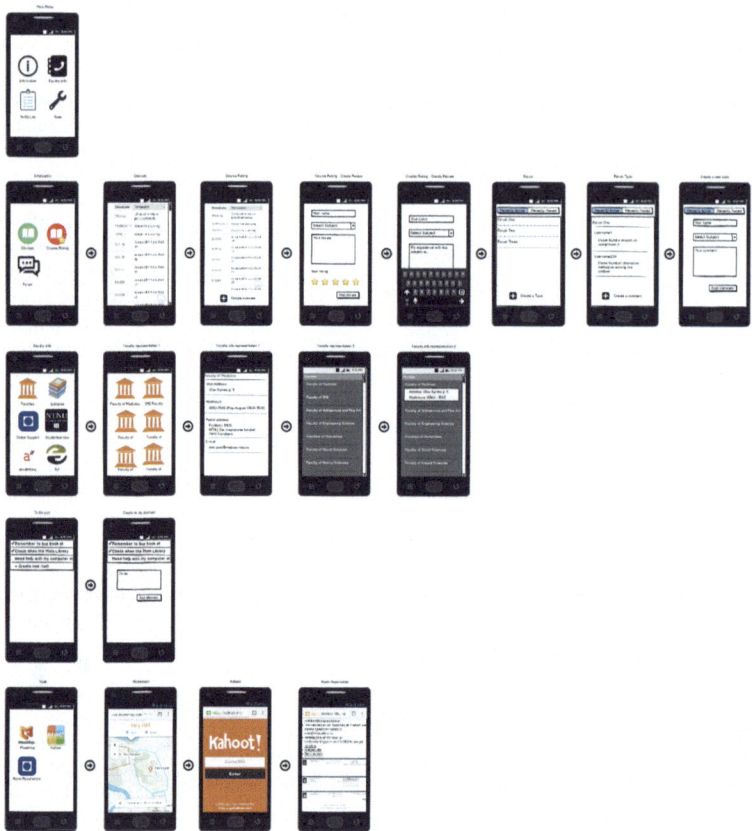

Fig. 3.4 Final user interfaces (wireframes) of a mobile learning application. (Adapted from Pappas et al., 2017, with permission by IEEE)

3.2 Artifacts and Treatment Design

One of the first notions the researcher needs to understand in learning technology and CCI research (and also in neighboring fields) is the unit of analysis (UoA). The UoA is the object that is the target of the experimentation (and whose data we use as a unit in our analysis). The UoA can be an individual, a small group, an organization (a school), or the users of certain technology. For instance, if we are interested in studying the effect of the use of a dashboard or a representation (an avatar) on students' learning outcomes or attitudes, then the UoA is the student, since we will use the score of each student. If we want to study the introduction of novel technology to support collaboration in dyads or triads, the UoA is the dyad or triad, since we will use the score of each dyad or triad (e.g., scores from a common assignment). Even objects can serve as a UoA; if we want to make an interface more attractive to students, then the UoA is the group of students who use the interface. Identifying the UoA can be complex, as it is not always static. It is common in a study with a specific dataset to have different UoAs. For example, an analysis of student scores can be based on the scores of individuals, of classes (if we want to compare the practice of different teachers), or of different groups.

Another important concept that is a cornerstone in learning technology and CCI research (and also in neighboring fields) is that of "artifact" (or "artefact" in British English spelling) (Carroll & Rosson, 1992). Artifacts correspond to novel designs (which may be prototype systems, interfaces, materials, or procedures) that have a certain set of qualities or components (such as functionalities and affordances) and that allow us to experiment (e.g., to isolate and test certain components). Such experimentation serves to advance both empirical and theoretical knowledge, but it also supports the practice of a user (such as a learner or a child) and empowers them to achieve their potential. Artifacts allow us to formulate the necessary conditions by isolating certain functionalities and testing our hypotheses through experimentation. Each experimental study has its own value and should contribute to the main body of knowledge by validly testing theories that are contingent on designed artifacts, or by producing findings that may be reused to support the design of future artifacts in the form of lessons learned or design implications (Sutcliffe, 2000).

Contemporary learning technology and CCI research focuses on conducting "artifact-centered evaluations" that use artifacts in the experimental process. The most common approaches cascade the experimentation process within a broader research procedure, with the intention of producing new knowledge and models and informing theories and practices. Such approaches inherit the characteristics of design research and are iterative. For instance, design-based research (DBR) is a common approach in learning technology, whereas the task–artefact cycle is commonly employed in HCI (see Fig. 3.5). Such research approaches are important, as they go beyond responding to a particular hypothesis, instead seeking to advance theoretical knowledge in the field by exploring and confirming various hypotheses and relationships in different contexts (see a representation in Fig. 3.6).

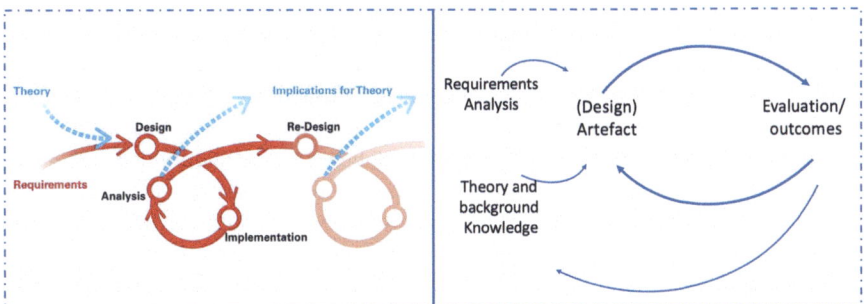

Fig. 3.5 Representations of common experimental processes. Left: Design-based research (DBR) research, which is commonly used in learning technology research (Barab & Squire, 2004). Right: The task–artefact cycle, which is commonly used in interaction design research. (Adapted from Carroll & Rosson, 1992; Sutcliffe, 2000). Both processes are iterative in nature and focus on producing practical and theoretical knowledge

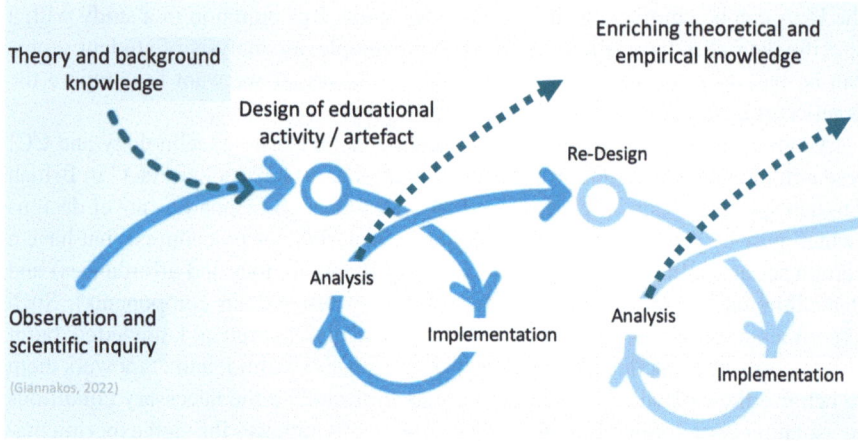

Fig. 3.6 Iterative design research focusing on producing empirical and theoretical knowledge

Going back to the important role of artifacts in conducting empirical studies, we now provide some examples of how artifacts allow us to move from observations to designing treatments and testing hypotheses. A very common interface in learning technology research is the dashboard. Dashboards are used in learning management systems (LMSs) such as Canvas, Moodle and Blackboard Learn, and also in the majority of learning technologies (e.g., digital games, educational apps). Although there are differences in the information included, the visualizations employed, and the moments at which the dashboard appears, most dashboards include information related to learners' activity, progress, and learning history. The information provided to the learner (and teacher) is intended to activate their awareness, reflection, and judgment (i.e., metacognition), and ultimately to support their potential (by informing them about the amount of time spent on a task, the difficulty of a particular question, and so on). Providing this information in an efficient manner will support learners' self-regulation and motivation, and teachers learning design and decision making, allowing them to make appropriate decisions about allocation of effort, time-management, and skills development (Lonn et al., 2015).

Figure 3.7 (up) shows a learning dashboard, taken from a previously introduced example (Westermoen & Lunde, 2020), this dashboard has been designed and introduced to support students' self-assessment. The dashboard was introduced to one of two groups of students, and a mixed methods study was conducted to investigate the role of the dashboard in digital self-assessment activities (Westermoen & Lunde, 2020; Papamitsiou et al., 2021). Fig. 3.7 (down) shows a teacher dashboard, this dashboard has been designed and introduced to support teachers' decision making (e.g., identifying students' weaknesses and misconceptions, or students who need additional support). The dashboard was evaluated with experienced teachers to identify its usefulness and ability to support decision making and instruction (Luick & Monsen, 2022).

3.2 Artifacts and Treatment Design

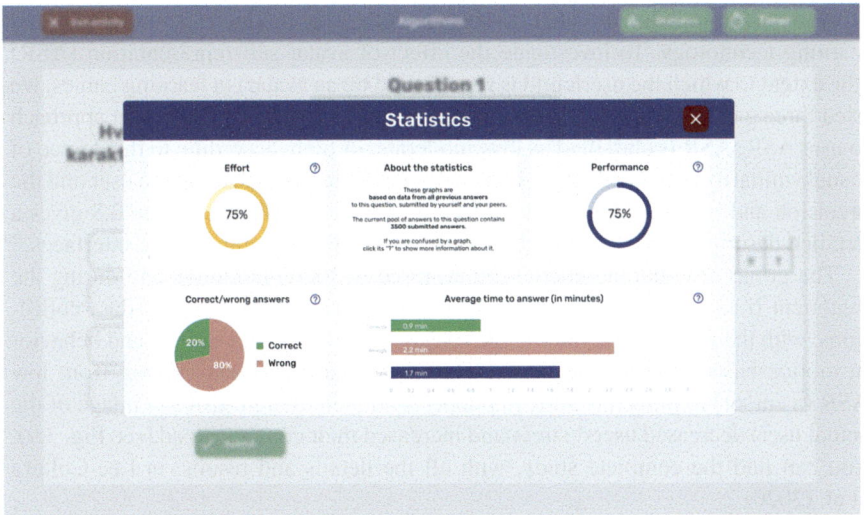

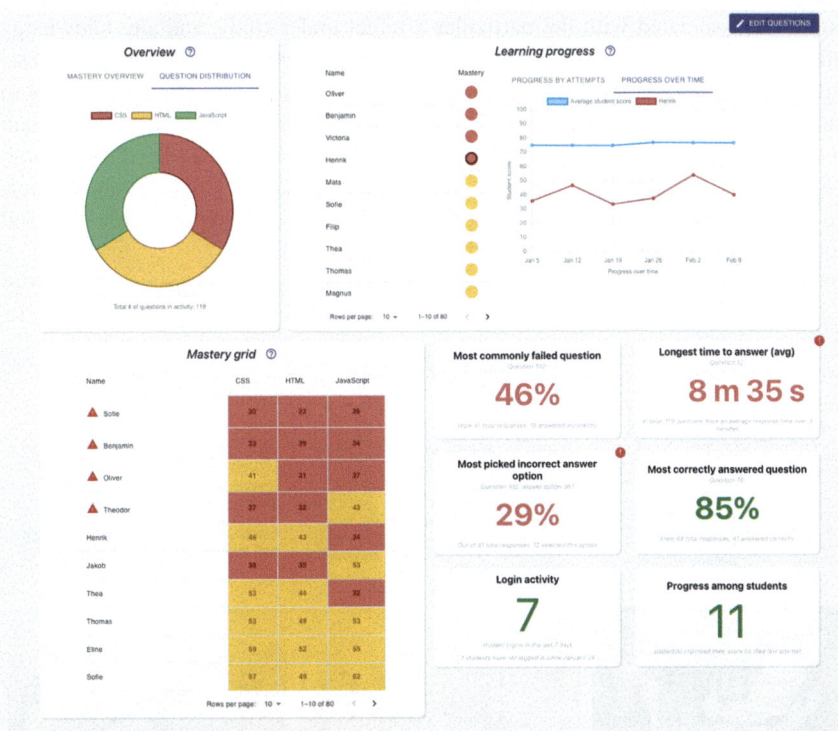

Fig. 3.7 Up: Student dashboard with task-related analytics for each question. (From Westermoen & Lunde, 2020; with permission by Westermoen and Lunde); Down: teacher dashboard with task-related analytics for the whole class and course. (From Luick & Monsen, 2022; with permission by Luick and Monsen)

Another example is provided by artifacts that lie at the intersection of CCI and learning technology. To investigate the effect of avatar self-representation (ASR) (the extent to which the user/child is represented by an avatar) in learning games, we used three games that follow similar game mechanics but have a different approach to user ASR. ASR is classified as low, moderate, or high, according to the degree of visual similarity (i.e., appearance congruity) between the avatar and the user and the precision and breadth of movement (i.e., movement congruity). Figure 3.8 gives a detailed description of the ASR classifications and the respective game interfaces.

The group of children experienced all three ASRs (conditions), and during the treatment (i.e., a within-subjects experiment) we carried out various data collections, with the goal of determining the role of ASR in children's affect and behavior in motion-based educational games. The results indicated that moving from low ASR (a cursor) to moderate ASR (a puppet) and then to high ASR (an image of the actual user) decreased users' stress and increased their cognitive load (see Fig. 3.9). You can find the complete study, with all the details and results, in Lee-Cultura et al. (2020).

The use of artifacts is powerful, but it also has limitations. For example, the results are associated with the particular artefact under study, and any knowledge obtained is not necessarily reusable or generalizable to other contexts. Nevertheless, artifacts allow us to conduct experiments and test hypotheses efficiently so as to enhance relevant practical and theoretical knowledge. In addition, there are certain time-tested approaches in both learning technology and CCI/HCI (e.g., DBR; Barab & Squire, 2004) and the task–artefact cycle (Sutcliffe, 2000) that allow us to leverage iterative experimentation to go beyond context-specific hypothesis testing and produce reusable/generalizable knowledge.

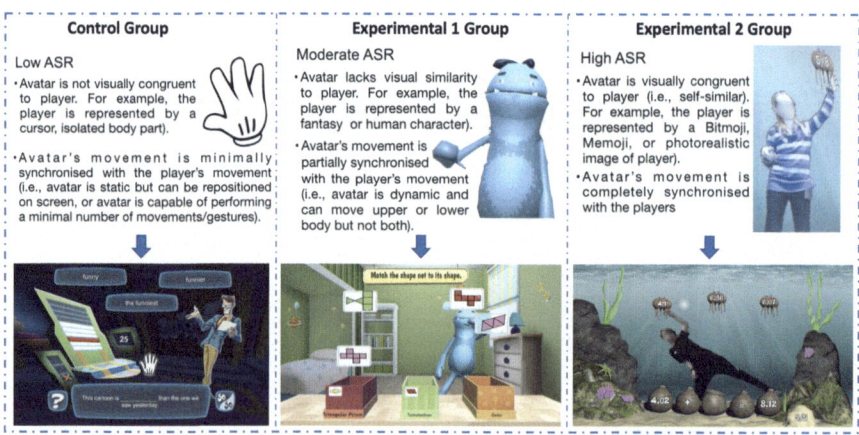

Fig. 3.8 Artifacts corresponding to three different degrees of avatar self-representation (ASR). (Adapted from Lee-Cultura et al., 2020, with permission by Lee-Cultura)

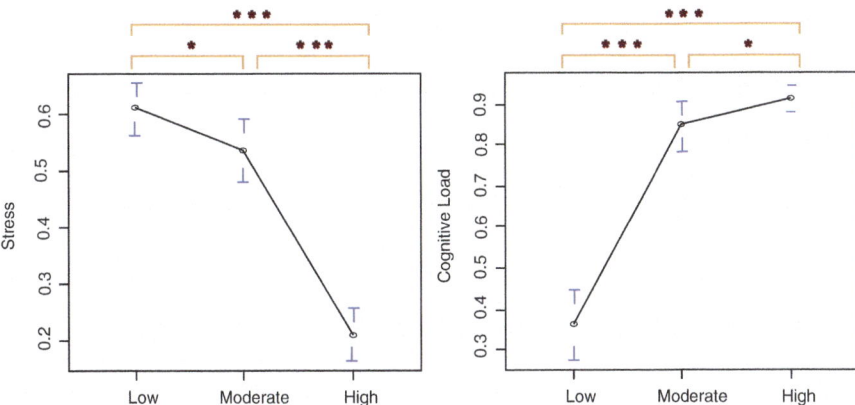

Fig. 3.9 Indicative results of the ASR study. (Adapted from Lee-Cultura et al., 2020, with permission by Lee-Cultura). The blue bars show 95% confidence intervals. Statistically significant differences are marked with * for $p <= 0.05$, ** for $p <= 0.001$, and *** for $p <= 0.0001$

References

Asheim, J. (2012). *Konsept for forbedret behandling av barn rammet av astma/RS-virus* (Master's thesis, Institutt for produktdesign). http://hdl.handle.net/11250/241157.

Barab, S., & Squire, K. (2004). Design-based research: Putting a stake in the ground. *The Journal of the Learning Sciences, 13*(1), 1–14.

Branch, R. M. (2009). *Instructional design: The ADDIE approach* (Vol. 722). Springer Science & Business Media.

Bruner, J. S. (1960). *The process of education*. Oxford University Press.

Carroll, J. M., & Mack, R. L. (1985). Metaphor, computing systems, and active learning. *International Journal of Man-Machine Studies, 22*(1), 39–57.

Carroll, J. M., & Rosson, M. B. (1992). Getting around the task-artifact cycle: How to make claims and design by scenario. *ACM Transactions on Information Systems (TOIS), 10*(2), 181–212.

Cetusic, L. (2017). *Mobile learning ecosystem to enhance students learning-lessons learnt from an empirical study at NTNU* (Master's thesis, NTNU). https://ntnuopen.ntnu.no/ntnu-xmlui/handle/11250/2442324

DiSalvo, B., Yip, J., Bonsignore, E., & Carl, D. (2017). *Participatory design for learning* (pp. 3–6). Routledge.

Høiseth, M., Giannakos, M. N., Alsos, O. A., Jaccheri, L., & Asheim, J. (2013). Designing healthcare games and applications for toddlers. In *Proceedings of the 12th international conference on interaction design and children* (pp. 137–146).

Kuhn, W., & Blumenthal, B. (1996). Spatialization: Spatial metaphors for user interfaces. In *Conference companion on human factors in computing systems* (pp. 346–347).

Lee-Cultura, S., Sharma, K., Papavlasopoulou, S., Retalis, S., & Giannakos, M. (2020). Using sensing technologies to explain children's self-representation in motion-based educational games. In *Proceedings of the interaction design and children conference* (pp. 541–555).

Lonn, S., Aguilar, S. J., & Teasley, S. D. (2015). Investigating student motivation in the context of a learning analytics intervention during a summer bridge program. *Computers in Human Behavior, 47*, 90–97.

Luick, A., & Monsen, F. (2022). *Adaptive teaching technologies to create and monitor learning activities* (Master's thesis), NTNU.

Neale, D. C., & Carroll, J. M. (1997). The role of metaphors in user interface design. In M. G. Helander, T. K. Landauer, & P. V. Prabhu (Eds.), *Handbook of human-computer interaction* (pp. 441–462). North-Holland.

Noor, J. (2016). *Pervasively gamifying the museum experience-an empirical investigation of knowledge gain and engagement* (Master's thesis), NTNU. https://ntnuopen.ntnu.no/ntnu-xmlui/handle/11250/2442326

Papamitsiou, Z., Lunde, M., Westermoen, J., & Giannakos, M. N. (2021). Supporting learners in a crisis context with smart self-assessment. In D. Burgos, A. Tlili, & A. Tabacco (Eds.), *Radical solutions for education in a crisis context* (pp. 207–224). Springer.

Pappas, I. O., Cetusic, L., Giannakos, M. N., & Jaccheri, L. (2017). Mobile learning adoption through the lens of complexity theory and fsQCA. In *2017 IEEE global engineering education conference (EDUCON)* (pp. 536–541). IEEE.

Sharma, K., Leftheriotis, I., & Giannakos, M. (2020). Utilizing interactive surfaces to enhance learning, collaboration and engagement: Insights from learners' gaze and speech. *Sensors, 20*(7), 1964.

Streitz, N. A. (1988). Mental models and metaphors: Implications for the design of adaptive user-system interfaces. In *Learning issues for intelligent tutoring systems* (pp. 164–186). Springer.

Sutcliffe, A. (2000). On the effective use and reuse of HCI knowledge. *ACM Transactions on Computer-Human Interaction (TOCHI), 7*(2), 197–221.

Westermoen, J., & Lunde, M. (2020). *Smartu investigating the effects of visualizations in adaptive self assessment systems* (Master's thesis), NTNU. https://ntnuopen.ntnu.no/ntnu-xmlui/handle/11250/2777507

Wilson, J., & Rosenberg, D. (1988). Rapid prototyping for user interface design. In M. G. Helander, T. K. Landauer, & P. V. Prabhu (Eds.), *Handbook of human-computer interaction* (pp. 859–875). North-Holland.

Open Access This chapter is licensed under the terms of the Creative Commons Attribution 4.0 International License (http://creativecommons.org/licenses/by/4.0/), which permits use, sharing, adaptation, distribution and reproduction in any medium or format, as long as you give appropriate credit to the original author(s) and the source, provide a link to the Creative Commons license and indicate if changes were made.

The images or other third party material in this chapter are included in the chapter's Creative Commons license, unless indicated otherwise in a credit line to the material. If material is not included in the chapter's Creative Commons license and your intended use is not permitted by statutory regulation or exceeds the permitted use, you will need to obtain permission directly from the copyright holder.

Chapter 4
Educational Data, Learning Analytics and Dashboards

Abstract When learners interact with technologies and the learning context, a large amount of data is created. The collection, analysis, and utilization of those educational data has provided opportunities for learning technology (and CCI) research. In this chapter, we will discuss how learning systems produce and utilize educational data. In particular, we will discuss contemporary developments in the fields of learning analytics, educational data mining, and learner modelling; and how those advancements have impacted the design and functionalities of learning technologies.

Keywords Educational data · Learning dashboards · Learning technology · Learning analytics

4.1 Educational Data and Learning Analytics

In the second chapter, we introduced the notion of learning analytics, a central concept of which is the "learning trace," or, more generally speaking, the "user trace." Those traces are left behind when learners interact with technologies and the learning context in general (e.g., other learners, an instructor, or nondigital learning materials), and are represented by different datasets. Learner interaction is often complex (e.g., watching a video or answering a multiple-choice question), and traditional analytics model those interactions as a sequence of logs (e.g., video navigation, response times, and response correctness). These learning traces and the respective representations (visualizations, graphs, or diagrams) are used to improve the system's functionalities and intelligence (through, for example, recommender systems or visualization of an individual's progress) and the respective pedagogy, allowing learners and teachers to be aware of the possible misunderstandings and challenges associated with different content areas. Figure 4.1 depicts how typical use of learning systems (from instructors and learners) produce data that are processed from data analysis methods with an ultimate goal to support learning and instruction.

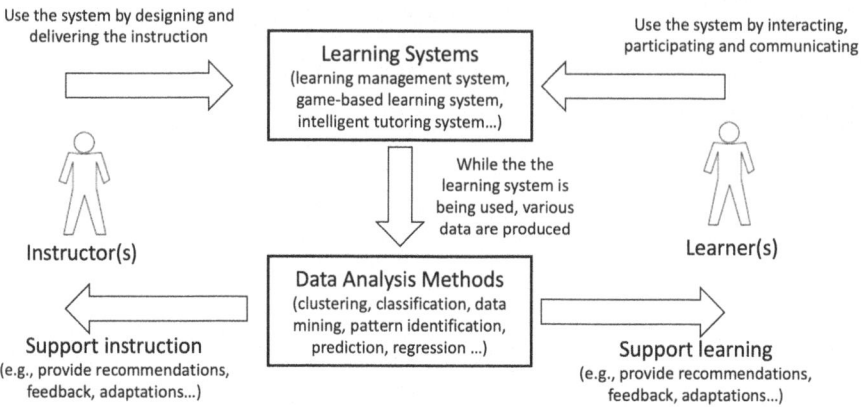

Fig. 4.1 Typical use of a learning system from the instructor and the learner, and the production of data that can support the learning and instruction

The datasets employed in learning technology platforms usually follow standards such as the sharable content object reference model or SCORM (SCORM, 2004) or other standardized data structures and formats. SCORM is the most widely used specification, with the goal of interoperability and smooth data and content exchange between learning technologies. Most LMSs use (or are at the very least compliant with) SCORM, which has its origins in a cooperation between the Institute of Electrical and Electronic Engineers (IEEE) Learning Technology Standards Committee (https://ltsc.ieee.org/), the IMS Global Learning Consortium (www.IMSproject.org), and the Alliance of Remote Instructional Authoring and Distribution Networks for Europe (ARIADNE). Independently of the standards employed, educational data also employ data structures in various formats, such as JavaScript object notation (JSON), extensible markup language (XML), or comma-separated values (CSV), which enable both the system and the researcher to carry out visualization and analysis. For example, you can find here[1] example events exemplify how you can utilize learners' tracking logs, those examples are from edX (an American MOOC provider created by Harvard and MIT), edX has an open-source platform (open edX) that powers edX courses. Those events (edX.log files) have no personally identifiable information, but exemplify how they can help us to gain insight into leaners and teachers. Learning interaction data sometimes might be provided in a relatively "primitive" form (the same applies for edX), however, there are several technological tools, such as HarvardX Tools (developed from Jim Waldo, see here: http://github.com/jimwaldo/HarvardX-Tools) that allow us to package, analyze, and manipulate by converting tracking log data to standard and manageable formats (e.g., csv based on ADL's xAPI (https://adlnet.gov/projects/xapi/)). Another useful resource is the Pittsburgh Science of Learning Center's DataShop

---

[1] EdX guide: https://edx.readthedocs.io/projects/devdata/en/stable/internal_data_formats/tracking_logs.html

(https://pslcdatashop.web.cmu.edu/) that hosts datasets from learning systems (most of them are from Intelligent Tutoring Systems) and provide them as a service to the learning technology community (e.g., so researchers can store or request and research on learning interaction data).

Learning analytics are then utilizing learning traces via the respective produced datasets to exploit opportunities for improving learning and instruction, to do so learning analytics employ computational analysis techniques coming from data science and AI. The majority of the learning analytics studies utilize descriptive statistics and basic visualization techniques (Fig. 4.2). For example, frequencies (the number of times a particular score or value is found in the data set), percentages (a set of scores or values as a percentage of the whole), means (numerical average of the scores or values for a particular variable) and medians (the numerical midpoint of the scores or values that is at the center of the distribution of the scores) are used often to support learners and instructors. Other statistical techniques such as correlational and regression analysis are also used, however, there are limited studies employing advanced data analysis methods in the context of learning analytics. Figure 4.2 categorizes the results from a literature review conducted from Misiejuk and Wasson (2017), that depict the frequency of the data analysis methods used. Moreover, Fig. 4.3 summarizes the advanced computational analysis techniques that can be used to support learning (Daud et al., 2017). The comparison indicates that learning analytics research and practice makes use of advanced computational analysis techniques, but to a limited extend (this indicates the status until 2017). Although this might connect with researchers' preferences, experience and aspirations; this might also connect with the fact that basic descriptive statistics (e.g., median, mean, frequency) might be easier for the end-users (e.g., students, teachers) to sense-make and act upon.

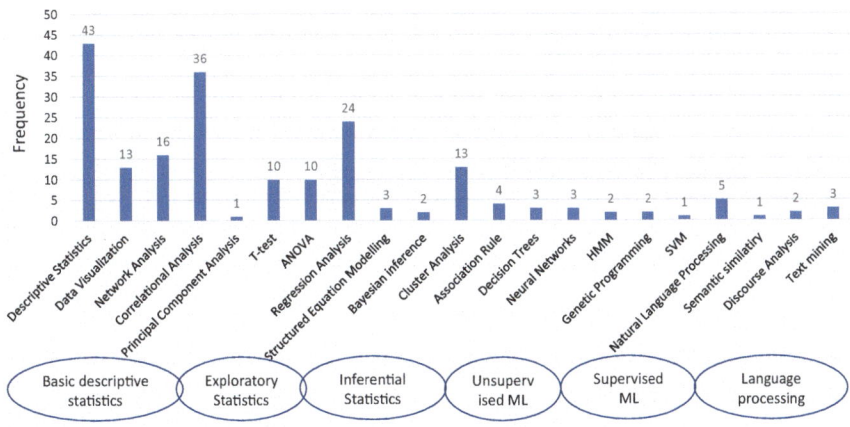

Fig. 4.2 Frequency of the data analysis methods used in the context of learning analytics research. (Source data came from Misiejuk & Wasson, 2017)

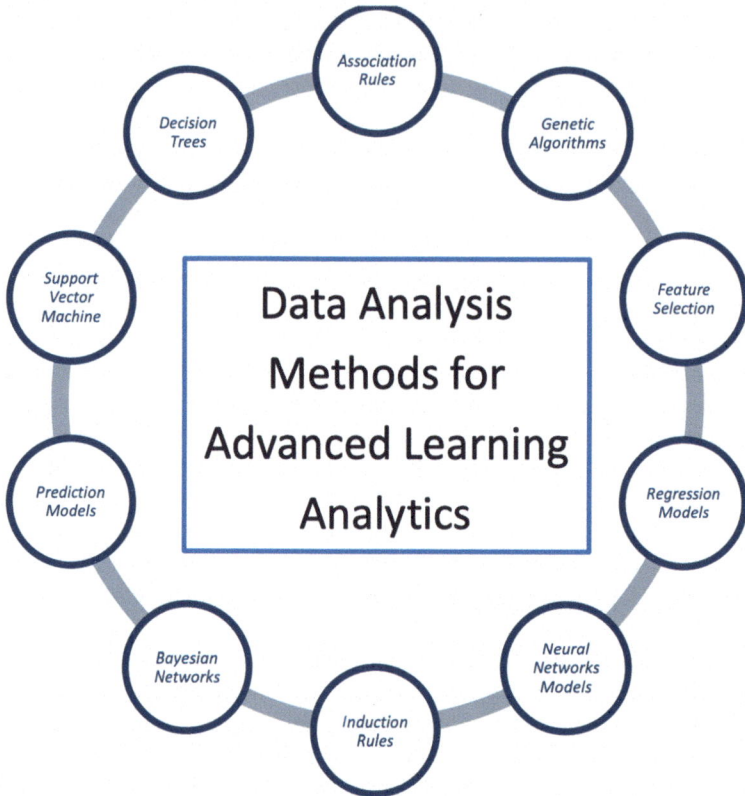

Fig. 4.3 Summary of the advanced computational analysis techniques that can be used. (Adapted from Daud et al., 2017; licensed under CC BY-ND 4.0)

4.2 Learner Modeling

In the process of standardizing how this information can be used to support the system (e.g., by providing intelligence) or the users (e.g., students and teachers), learning technology research came up with the term "learner model" (or "student model") (Bull, 2020). Learner modeling stems from user modeling, which describes the process of building and updating a conceptual understanding of the user (Fischer, 2001); by analogy, *a learner model describes the process of building and updating a conceptual understanding of the user as a learner.* To do this, it models attributes such as skills, competences, understanding of concepts, and misconceptions, as well as noncognitive attributes such as motivation, engagement, and effort (Bull, 2020). Learner models use a range of data, including response time, response correctness, number of attempts to solve a problem, time spent interacting with learning resources, navigation to various learning resources, activity on the various communication functionalities (e.g., forums), and other learning trace data (Bull, 2020). Learner models are (usually) automatically and dynamically generated and updated

4.2 Learner Modeling

(that is, inferred from the data). However, there are models that use manual input from learners' records or the teacher. The main objective of the learner model is to enable the learning system's intelligence and system functionalities (e.g., personalized learning, recommender systems, dashboards, and adaptivity) to support end-users, be they children, students, teachers, or parents. Bull and Kay (2010) provide several examples of learner models designed to support various users, including children, peers, parents and teacher.

Such functionalities allow technologies to support learners' educational needs, with learner models being a core component in the development of several learning technologies, such as MOOCs (e.g., Cook et al., 2015), LMSs (e.g., Chou et al., 2015), and, in particular, intelligent tutoring systems (ITSs) (Woolf, 2010). During the last years, we have mainly seen open learner models, which externalize their functionalities in a way that allows users to interpret them through, for example, visualizations. In addition, there are several open source tools that allow us to include such functionalities in our systems, such as the open learner model (OLM) application, developed by Susan Bull in the context of an EU project called Next-Tell (http://next-tell.eu/portfolios/olm/). Learner models visualize individual learners' current understanding (knowledge mastery) of a topic (see Fig. 4.4 for

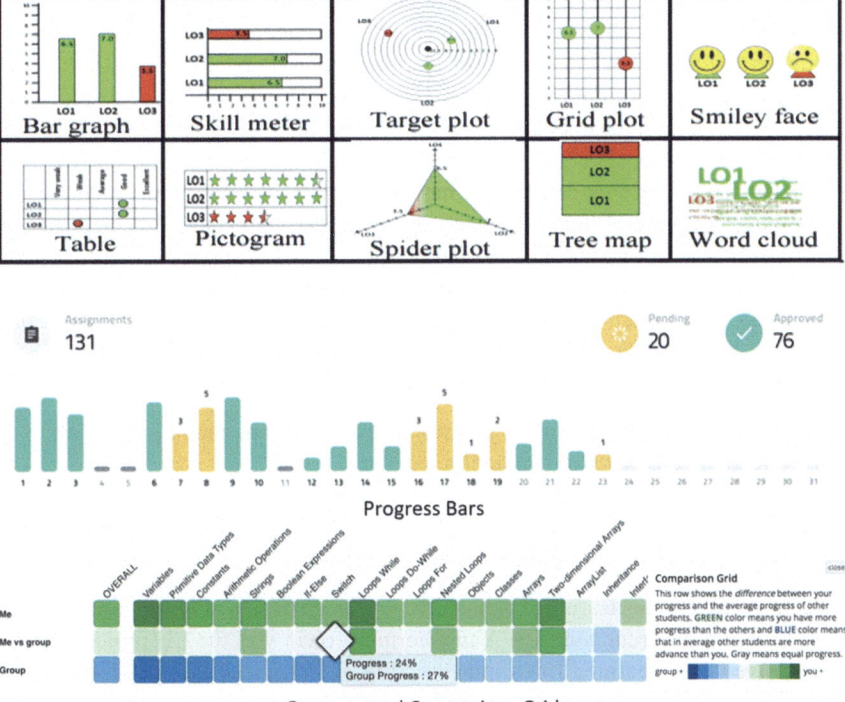

Fig. 4.4 Learner modelling tools that visualize individual (or group) learners' current understanding of a topic or their level of competency, and support different processes (e.g., following progress, comparison, identifying misconceptions)

some examples). These models are powered automatically from a variety of sources, and they visualize the most up-to-date information about learner competency to allow learners and instructors to identify strengths and areas for further attention.

4.3 Educational Dashboards and Visualization

For the end-users of learning technologies (learners, teachers, and administrators), it is extremely useful to have information presented in an understandable way that supports their objectives of learning, teaching, or making administrative decisions about learning and teaching. Visualizations such as charts, graphs, and maps provide accessible ways to see and understand useful trends and patterns in the data. However, a single chart, graph, or map cannot contain all the information and insights needed to support end-users' informed decision making. The solution is to use combined information visualization techniques with the use of a dashboard, so that the different end-users no longer need to "drive blind" (Duval, 2011).

In the literature, dashboards have been defined as "an easy to read, often single-page, real-time user interface, showing a graphical presentation of the current status (snapshot) and historical trends of an organizations key performance indicators (KPIs) to enable instantaneous and informed decisions to be made at a glance" (Brouns et al., 2015). In the context of learning technology, a learning dashboard has been defined in the context of a recent literature review as "a single display that aggregates different indicators about learner(s), learning process(es) and/or learning context(s) into one or multiple visualizations" (Schwendimann et al., 2016). The design and use of learning dashboards has increased tremendously in recent years, but there are still several important decisions that need to be made by the designer of the dashboard. For instance, what is the "right" information to visualize for the different end-user groups? How does this information need to be visualized, in which part of the system (which UI), and at which point of use (which part of the storyline)? Although there is unlikely to be a single answer for every learning dashboard, it is important to consider five main points:

1. the purpose of the dashboard (e.g., awareness, reflection, and/or guidance);
2. the intended end-user (student and/or teacher);
3. the educational data available;
4. the affordances of the technology involved (e.g., LMSs, games, and MOOCs); and
5. the context of use (e.g., the university context).

In recent years, various learning dashboards have been designed to support teaching and learning in different contexts. A pioneering project was the EU project ROLE (Responsive Open Learning Environments). Fig. 4.5 provides a range of visualizations employed: (a) in the context of the ROLE project (Santos et al., 2011) and (b) in the context of the work from Luick & Monsen (2022) (10 years later). In line with the first principle of designing a learning dashboard (that it be purposeful), we can easily identify the goal for these different visualizations. For instance, we can see

4.3 Educational Dashboards and Visualization

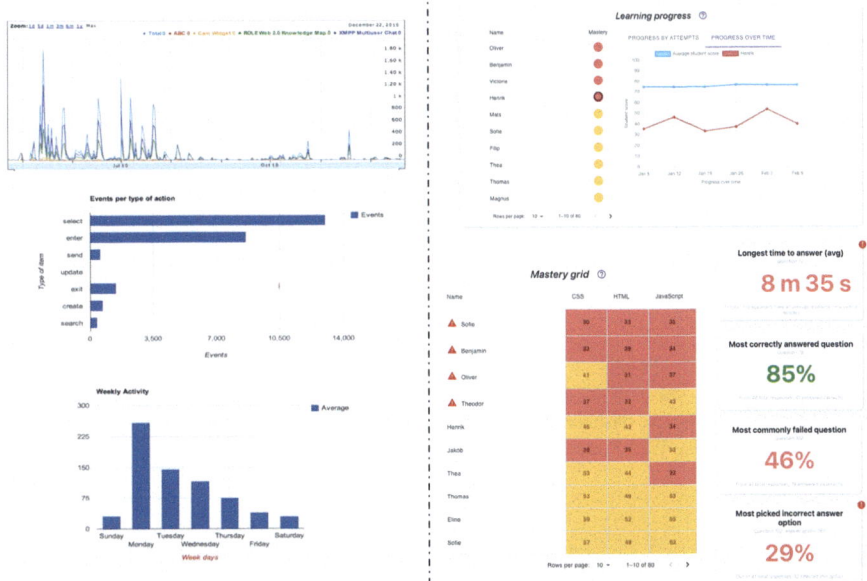

Fig. 4.5 Left: elements of a teacher dashboard designed in the context of the EU ROLE project. (Adapted from Santos et al., 2011; licensed under CC BY-ND 4.0); Right: elements of a teacher dashboard. (Adapted from Luick & Monsen, 2022; with permission by Luick and Monsen)

that most of the students were most active in the period May–July (top-left visualization), that they entered chatrooms much more often than they posted messages (second and third line in middle-left visualization), and that the most "productive" was Monday (bottom-left visualization). In another project conducted at NTNU 10 years later, by Luick & Monsen (2022), we see dashboards that allow teachers to follow students' progress over time (up-right visualization in Fig. 4.5), across different topics of a course and providing insights about the learning content (bottom-right visualization in Fig. 4.5). Such information can help students to reflect on the activities they engage with and the behaviors they exhibit. It can also help the teacher to reorganize and/or redesign the learning activities in a way that is more engaging for the students, and focus on topics that are difficult to master.

Recent developments in the design of learning dashboards have incorporated capabilities such as social comparison (where individuals can see their own KPIs together with the cumulative KPIs of the classroom/group), with the goal of supporting self-regulated learning and student engagement. One example is Mastery Grids, which uses learners' data to provide interactive and adaptive visualizations that support their engagement, performance, and motivation (Guerra et al., 2016). Mastery Grids combines open learner model with social comparison, with an ultimate goal to enable the learner to be aware of their own strength and weakness, and empower them. It compares learners' knowledge level (mastery) by colored grids as shown in Fig. 4.6. The four levels portray: student's progress ("Me"), a comparison between the user and other learner in the group ("Me vs group"), group level

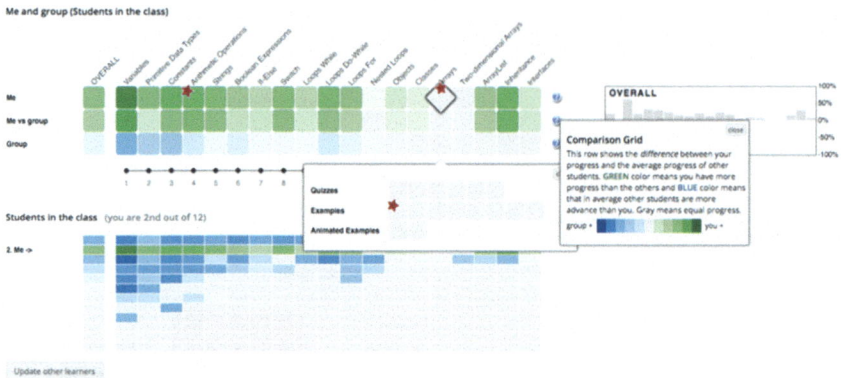

Fig. 4.6 Mastery Grids dashboard visualizing learners' knowledge and progress. (Source: Personalized Adaptive Web Systems Lab)

Fig. 4.7 A learning dashboard that supports social comparison, designed in the context of ProTuS. (From Vesin et al., 2018; licensed under CC BY-ND 4.0)

progress ("Group"), and overall progress of the learners in the class. Mastery Grids was developed in the Personalized Adaptive Web Systems Lab of the University of Pittsburgh, and is openly available to everyone (see: http://adapt2.sis.pitt.edu/wiki/Mastery_Grids_Interface).

Another example has been implemented in the context of the Programming Tutoring System (ProTuS). It allows students to see how they have performed in the different parts of the course compared to their colleagues in the classroom (see Fig. 4.7). The dashboard uses the results from various quizzes associated with different areas of the content of the course. The ProTuS interface and the analytics component has been employed in the web technologies course at the Norwegian University of Science and Technologies (Vesin et al., 2018).

Research on the design, development and use of learning dashboards is at the forefront of both learning technology and CCI. With contemporary research suggesting that future generation of learning dashboards need to be actionable, tailored to the needs of end-users, responsible, configurable, interactive, integrated and embedded in both the learning and visual sciences (Verbert et al., 2020).

References

Brouns, F., et al. (2015). *D2.5 learning analytics requirements and metrics report* [online]. https://repositorio.unican.es/xmlui/handle/10902/15231.
Bull, S. (2020). There are open learner models about! *IEEE Transactions on Learning Technologies, 13*(2), 425–448.
Bull, S., & Kay, J. (2010). Open learner models. In *Advances in intelligent tutoring systems* (pp. 301–322). Springer.
Chou, C. Y., Tseng, S. F., Chih, W. C., Chen, Z. H., Chao, P. Y., Lai, K. R., et al. (2015). Open student models of core competencies at the curriculum level: Using learning analytics for student reflection. *IEEE Transactions on Emerging Topics in Computing, 5*(1), 32–44.
Cook, R., Kay, J., & Kummerfeld, B. (2015). MOOClm: User modelling for MOOCs. In *International conference on user modeling, adaptation, and personalization* (pp. 80–91). Springer.
Daud, A., Aljohani, N. R., Abbasi, R. A., Lytras, M. D., Abbas, F., & Alowibdi, J. S. (2017). Predicting student performance using advanced learning analytics. In *Proceedings of the 26th international conference on world wide web companion* (pp. 415–421).
Duval, E. (2011). Attention please! Learning analytics for visualization and recommendation. In *Proceedings of the 1st international conference on learning analytics and knowledge* (pp. 9–17).
Fischer, G. (2001). User modeling in human–computer interaction. *User Modeling and User-Adapted Interaction, 11*(1), 65–86.
Guerra, J., Hosseini, R., Somyurek, S., & Brusilovsky, P. (2016). An intelligent interface for learning content: Combining an open learner model and social comparison to support self-regulated learning and engagement. In *Proceedings of the 21st international conference on intelligent user interfaces* (pp. 152–163).
Luick, A., & Monsen, F. (2022). *Teaching dashboard* (Master's thesis), NTNU.
Misiejuk, K., & Wasson, B. (2017). *State of the field report on learning analytics*. Retrieved from http://bora.uib.no/handle/1956/17740.
Santos, J. L., Verbert, K., Govaerts, S., & Duval, E. (2011). Visualizing PLE usage. In *Proceedings of EFEPLE11 1st workshop on exploring the fitness and evolvability of personal learning environments* (Vol. 773, pp. 34–38).
Schwendimann, B. A., Rodriguez-Triana, M. J., Vozniuk, A., Prieto, L. P., Boroujeni, M. S., Holzer, A., et al. (2016). Perceiving learning at a glance: A systematic literature review of learning dashboard research. *IEEE Transactions on Learning Technologies, 10*(1), 30–41.
SCORM. (2004). *4th Edition Version 1.1 overview*. Retrieved December 09, 2021, from. https://adlnet.gov/projects/scorm/#scorm-2004-4th-edition
Verbert, K., Ochoa, X., De Croon, R., Dourado, R. A., & De Laet, T. (2020). Learning analytics dashboards: the past, the present and the future. In *Proceedings of the tenth international conference on learning analytics & knowledge* (pp. 35–40).

Vesin, B., Mangaroska, K., & Giannakos, M. (2018). Learning in smart environments: User-centered design and analytics of an adaptive learning system. *Smart Learning Environments, 5*(1), 1–21.

Woolf, B. P. (2010). Student modeling. In *Advances in intelligent tutoring systems* (pp. 267–279). Springer.

Open Access This chapter is licensed under the terms of the Creative Commons Attribution 4.0 International License (http://creativecommons.org/licenses/by/4.0/), which permits use, sharing, adaptation, distribution and reproduction in any medium or format, as long as you give appropriate credit to the original author(s) and the source, provide a link to the Creative Commons license and indicate if changes were made.

The images or other third party material in this chapter are included in the chapter's Creative Commons license, unless indicated otherwise in a credit line to the material. If material is not included in the chapter's Creative Commons license and your intended use is not permitted by statutory regulation or exceeds the permitted use, you will need to obtain permission directly from the copyright holder.

Chapter 5
Common Types of Experimental Designs in CCI and Learning Technology Research

Abstract Experiments and experimental studies are used to collect data and build scientific knowledge, and it is one of the primary methodologies for a wide range of disciplines including CCI and learning technology. In this chapter, we provide the basics of experimental research in CCI and learning technology. The goal is to support researchers to gain an understanding of the main methodological decisions and the ways in which experiments can answer RQs. Researchers will also be introduced in evaluating the circumstances that favour (or do not favour) the use of experiments, and how to make the necessary methodological decisions about the type and features of the experiment for CCI and learning technology research.

Keywords Experimental designs · Learning technology · Child-computer interaction

One of the main processed for evaluating an artifact (e.g., toward its indented use) and/or testing hypotheses on an artifact (e.g., UI, prototype, interaction technique) is experiment design. Experimental design is usually evaluating a particular system by means of statistical approaches. Detailed descriptions of experimental designs can be found in research textbooks and technical reports (e.g., Campbell & Stanley, 2015; McKenney & Reeves, 2018; Lazar et al., 2017; Cohen et al., 2002; MacKenzie, 2012). For the purposes of this book, we discuss four common experimental designs that CCI and learning technology researchers are likely to employ for their studies. These designs are considered "backbone" designs, in the sense that they leverage the core components that can be used to construct more complex designs. Therefore, understanding these four designs and their components will allow any CCI and learning technology researcher to also understand more complex designs, as well as to adapt and expand them to accommodate their needs.

Before moving on to the four designs, we would like to explain two core notions that will allow you to better understand them. Those two notions (or designs) are "between-subjects" (also known as "between-groups") and "within-subjects" (also "within-groups"). The notion of between-subjects is very common, and because of its roots in clinical trials, it is considered to be the gold standard of experimental research, especially when combined with random assignment of groups. The main idea is that each subject (e.g., a learner or a child) is exposed to only one condition, either the control condition or an experimental condition. Afterwards, statistical analysis investigates the difference in the variable of interest between the control group and the experimental group(s). The notion of within-subjects entails that each subject is assigned to all the treatments, in a single or repeated manner and in a specified or unspecified order, depending on the needs and goals of the experiment. The main idea is that the same subject should be exposed to all the treatments, which allows them to serve as "their own control group." Researchers can also combine those two designs in a mixed research design, which is, in effect, a within-subjects design inside a between-subjects design. This enables multiple comparisons but also increases the logistics and complexity of the study (which becomes, in effect, two studies). Such combinations and extensions of the basic research designs are not necessary for understanding the core designs, and are therefore beyond the scope of this note. Figure 5.1 shows how a simple experimental design with 12 participants and control and experimental conditions would look in the case of a between-subjects design, a within-subjects design, and a mixed design.

Those two notions are very powerful in CCI and learning technology research, and knowing their pros and cons allows researchers to make good choices. It is also important to highlight that there is no right or wrong research design. Instead, researchers should consider their needs (including contextual and disciplinary requirements) and make the most appropriate choice. Table 5.1 summarizes some common decision factors to bear in mind when considering the use of between- and within- subjects designs in CCI and learning technology research.

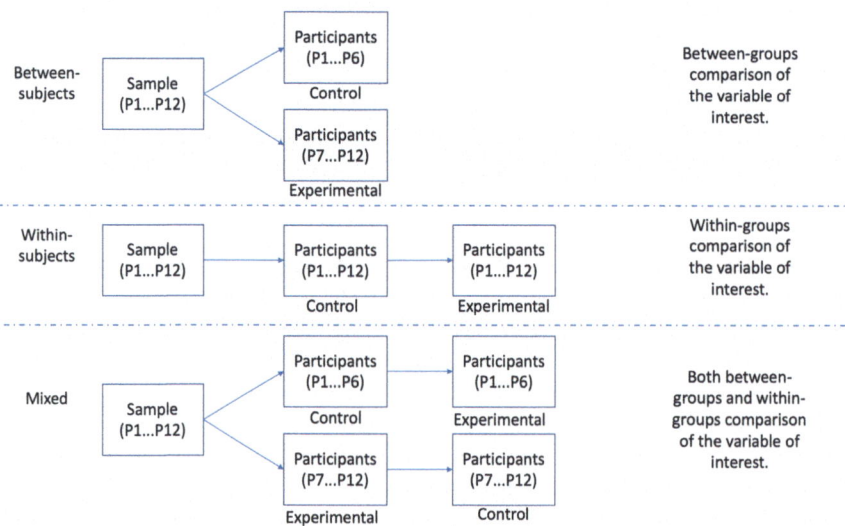

Fig. 5.1 A between-subjects design, a within-subjects design, and a mixed research design using the same sample of 12 participants.

5.1 Randomized (True) Experiments

Table 5.1 Decision factors for choosing a between-subjects design or a within-subjects design.

Between-subjects design	Within-subjects design
When the aim is to increase internal validity by eliminating any systematic error that might be associated with using intact groups	When it is not possible to perform randomized assignment to treatments (e.g., due to school restrictions)
When there are no differences or only small differences between subjects (e.g., reading speeds within a particular developmental stage) but large expected differences across conditions (e.g., reading on a small screen vs. reading on a big screen)	When there are large differences between the subjects (e.g., basic coding skills between children following different curricula)
When there are no ethical concerns with regard to offering the treatment to a selected population (e.g., no significant advantage or disadvantage over the control group population, or any such advantage is temporary)	When there are ethical concerns with regard to offering the treatment to a selected population (e.g., giving a significant advantage or disadvantage over the control group population, especially for a long period, such as a semester)
When learning and carry-over effects exist (e.g., mastering a task that is likely to have inherent benefits in relation to similar future tasks)	When learning and carry-over effects are unlikely to exist (e.g., mastering the task is unlikely to have inherent benefits in relation to similar future tasks)
When offering all treatments to all the subjects is impractical or impossible (e.g., in a longitudinal study), or the time of the study needs to be reduced (e.g., because of learner fatigue or difficulties in recruiting)	When the sample size is limited (e.g., due to restrictions, or because users are rare or hard to reach)

Now that we have explained those two core notions and their inherent qualities, we can distinguish four experimental designs that are commonly used in CCI and learning technology. These are also "backbone" designs in the sense that they can be used to construct more advanced designs. First, we consider randomized experiments (also known as "true experiments") that follow the between-subjects principles and use random assignment to create the control and experimental groups. Next, we consider quasi-experiments, which are mainly between-subjects (although you might see within-subjects experiments known as "repeated measures quasi-experiments"), with nonrandom assignment of subjects. The next design, repeated measures, is a within-subjects design in which all the subjects are exposed to all the conditions. Last, we consider the time series design, which is a quasi-experiment that employs repeated measurements, with the experimental condition(s) induced between the measurement periods. We will consider each of these designs in detail, but keep in mind that they constitute a basic set of research designs that are common in the fields of CCI and learning technology, and that they can be enhanced with "advanced qualities" such as counterbalancing, placebo confederates, and deceits, as required.

5.1 Randomized (True) Experiments

Randomized experiments are the ideal choice for maximizing the internal validity of a study. Their unique characteristic is that the subjects are assigned at random to a condition (the control group or the experimental group), which ensures that there are no significant differences between groups (Shadish et al., 2002). The random assignment eliminates any systematic error and ensures that the control and experimental groups are subjected to identical environmental conditions while being assigned to different conditions. This can be achieved by means of any random selection mechanism (e.g., a random numbers table, a random number generator app, or even tossing a fair coin).

A very simple example at the confluence of CCI and learning technology is a randomized experiment on the use of learning dashboards (i.e., a graphical user interface that visualizes students' activity) to support secondary school students. The aim is to identify any potential effect of the use of a dashboard (the independent/manipulated variable) on students' learning performance, such as their scores in weekly tests (the dependent/outcome variable). The students are assigned at random to either the control group (no use of dashboard) or the experimental group (use of dashboard). The experimental group is then exposed to the treatment (using the dashboard) for a period of time (e.g., 2 weeks). At the end of the period, we compare the learning performance scores of the two groups (Fig. 5.2).

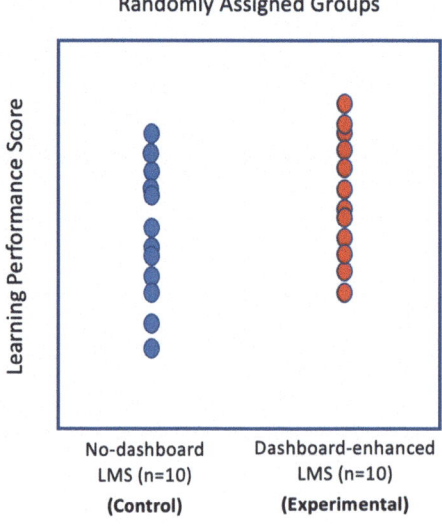

Fig. 5.2 Example of a randomized experiment

5.2 Quasi-Experiments

Quasi means "resembling," and quasi-experiments resemble experimental settings as far as possible without assigning subjects to conditions at random. Quasi-experiments allow the researcher to set the assignment of subjects to a control or experimental condition, depending on contextual factors, the ultimate goal, and any particular needs of the population in focus, according to some criterion (e.g., class, pre-test, or previous grades). In CCI and learning technology research, random assignment may be neither feasible nor practical, and in some cases it may not be ethical. A good example is research that occurs in school settings, where it is almost impossible to formulate random groups within a class environment and expose them to different conditions (and even if it is possible, it will result in very low ecological validity). Although such contextual factors preclude the use of randomized experiment, they lend themselves to the use of quasi-experiment. For instance, the researcher can expose two similar classes to the control and experimental conditions to identify the effect of the treatment (e.g., use of a technology) on the dependent variable (e.g., learning performance).

In a quasi-experiment, biases can easily be introduced. For example, schools may be included that have students with different socioeconomic statuses and different degrees of parental support; within a school, classrooms with different teachers or different curricula can be included. Accordingly, because of the lack of randomization, quasi-experiments face certain internal validity threats, and in many cases researchers use background information (e.g., students' grades or previous performance) or pretests (or even pre- and post-tests) to strengthen internal validity. These additional processes are used to establish group equivalence and to remedy the lack of the equivalence that true experiments obtain through randomization.

In terms of the previous example, a quasi-experiment will assign class A as the control group (no use of dashboard) and class B as the experimental group (use of dashboard). The researcher can also check the average grades between the two classes, or even conduct a pre-test to make sure that there is good group equivalence on the GPA. The experimental group is then exposed to the treatment (using the dashboard) for some time (e.g., 2 weeks). At the end of that period, the researcher can compare the learning performance scores of the two groups (Fig. 5.3).

5.3 Repeated Measures Experiments

A repeated measures design is a within-subjects design where all the participants are exposed to all the conditions. In practice, this means that each participant serves as their own control after being exposed to the treatment. In some cases, using the same sequence (e.g., control first, then experimental conditions) will work. Usually, however, a stronger design will involve randomizing or counterbalancing the order so as to eliminate any potential ordering effect. An example is when the participants

Fig. 5.3 Example of a quasi-experiment

2X2

G1	G2
A	B
B	A

3X3

G1	G2	G3
A	C	B
B	A	C
C	B	A

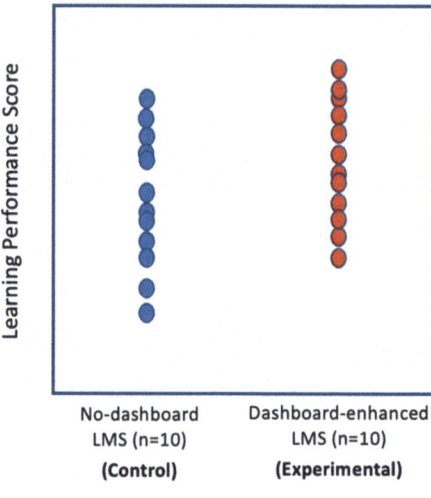

Fig. 5.4 Counterbalancing with two and three conditions (A, B and C are the conditions)

need to be exposed to the same learning materials, or when they are likely to get tired, as familiarity or fatigue might affect future learning performance. Thus, randomizing the order can help us to remove any potential order bias. Counterbalancing can also be used to deal with potential order effects while reducing potential carry-over effects. To achieve complete counterbalancing, we need to make sure that all the participants have been balanced across all the possible condition orders. With two conditions (control and experimental), this is a simple matter. However, when the number of conditions increases, counterbalancing becomes more complex (see Fig. 5.4), with the number of potential orderings growing at a cubic rate C^2 (with C being the number of conditions).

Returning to our previous example, a repeated measures study will expose all the participants to both conditions, probably in a randomized or counterbalanced way. For example, half of the participants will be exposed to the control condition first (no use of dashboard) and the other half to the experimental condition first (use of dashboard), and then this order will be reversed. At the end of the set period, the learning performance scores of the two groups will be compared (Fig. 5.5).

Fig. 5.5 Example of a repeated measures experiment

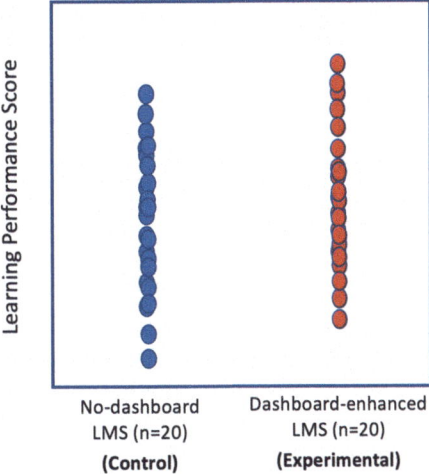

5.4 Time Series Experiments

The last type of experimental design we will consider in this chapter is the time series design, which involves repeated measurement of a group with the treatment (or treatments) induced. With the democratization of learning analytics and other user analytics (e.g., data collected from user clickstreams, keystrokes, or sensor data), this type of design is becoming more and more popular in contemporary learning technology and CCI research. The absence of randomization and distinct experimental and control groups (as in true experiments) entails all the difficulties associated with a quasi-experiment, not least the impossibility of attributing changes in the dependent variable directly to the treatment (since an improvement or deterioration in the performance of the group participating in the time series may be due to other factors, known as confounds). The uniqueness of this research design lies in the use of continuous measurements. In some cases (such as high-frequency learning analytics), this high frequency diminishes the introduction of confounding variables, many of which are introduced over time in learning technology and CCI contexts (e.g., familiarity with the task/content). Time series designs can take various forms, some of which provide better internal validity than others (e.g., multiple additions and deletions or switching replications; for more details, see Shadish et al., 2002). However, in order to conceptualize and understand this design, we can think of a single-group time series with group (G) and measurements (M) that take place several times prior to and after receiving the treatment (T).

G   M1   M2   T1   M3   M4   T2   M5   M6   ⊃

To better grasp this design, let us imagine that we have no dashboard as the control condition, dashboard type 1 as an experimental condition 1 (T1), and dashboard type 2 as another experimental condition 2 (T2). In the first time segment (e.g., a class hour or day), a group experiences the control condition, and the respective measurements (e.g., surveys or analytics) are taken. In the second time segment, the group experiences dashboard type 1, and again the respective measurements are taken. In the third time segment, the group experiences dashboard type 2, and again the respective measurements are taken. At the end of the period, as with the previous experimental designs, the measurements taken (e.g., learning performance scores) for the control and experimental groups are compared (Fig. 5.6). The time segments can be randomized and/or repeated, and other techniques can be applied that enable us to increase the internal validity.

A time series design is appropriate for longitudinal research designs and high-frequency data collections that involve a group or groups that are measured repeatedly, usually at regular intervals. It is important to remember that although time series design is a special type of quasi-experiment that takes advantage of the qualities of time (e.g., confounds that are introduced over time, altering/repeating conditions over time), it is also vulnerable to the weaknesses of quasi-experiments. Therefore, we should interpret the results with caution. Time series designs may also have specific weaknesses that must be addressed when analyzing the data. For example, they sometimes produce data points that are autocorrelated (for example, in very high-frequency data collection) and are therefore inadequate for certain statistical analyses (e.g., those that require independent data points; detailed information can be found in Kennedy, 1998). Conceptually, the primary concern is whether there is an exogenous influence (a confound variable) that takes place at the same time as any of the interventions (e.g., new or significantly different content, alterations to the instructions, or a bug in the system), or whether there are significant differences in the sample or an environmental condition (e.g., dropouts, fatigue, or changing classrooms).

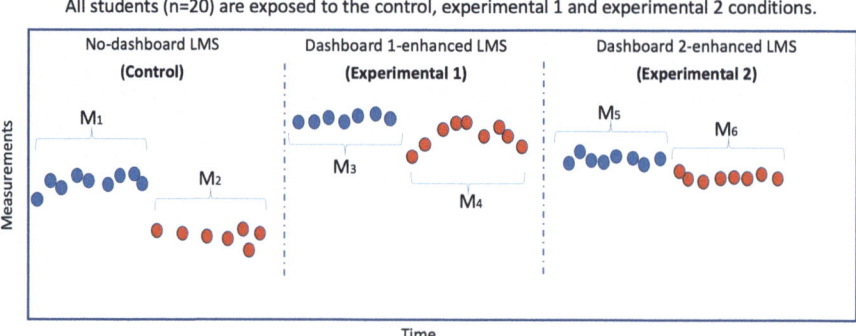

Fig. 5.6 Example of a time series experiment

In the past, time series design was mainly employed to detect unstable behavior patterns, and we see relatively few studies using this type of design (Ross & Morrison, 2013). Another reason for the limited use of this research design is the significant demands of longitudinal studies and prolonged involvement of human subjects. Moreover, we often find time series designs included under the umbrella term of "quasi-experimental design" (Campbell & Stanley, 2015).

References

Campbell, D. T., & Stanley, J. C. (2015). *Experimental and quasi-experimental designs for research*. Ravenio Books.
Cohen, L., Manion, L., & Morrison, K. (2002). *Research methods in education*. Routledge.
Kennedy, P. (1998). *A guide to econometrics*. The MIT Press.
Lazar, J., Feng, J. H., & Hochheiser, H. (2017). *Research methods in human-computer interaction*. Morgan Kaufmann.
MacKenzie, I. S. (2012). *Human-computer interaction: An empirical research perspective*. Morgan Kaufmann.
McKenney, S., & Reeves, T. C. (2018). *Conducting educational design research*. Routledge.
Ross, S. M., & Morrison, G. R. (2013). Experimental research methods. In *Handbook of research on educational communications and technology* (pp. 1007–1029). Routledge.
Shadish, W. R., Cook, T. D., & Campbell, D. T. (2002). *Experimental and quasi-experimental designs for generalized causal inference*. Houghton Mifflin.

Open Access This chapter is licensed under the terms of the Creative Commons Attribution 4.0 International License (http://creativecommons.org/licenses/by/4.0/), which permits use, sharing, adaptation, distribution and reproduction in any medium or format, as long as you give appropriate credit to the original author(s) and the source, provide a link to the Creative Commons license and indicate if changes were made.

The images or other third party material in this chapter are included in the chapter's Creative Commons license, unless indicated otherwise in a credit line to the material. If material is not included in the chapter's Creative Commons license and your intended use is not permitted by statutory regulation or exceeds the permitted use, you will need to obtain permission directly from the copyright holder.

Chapter 6
Data Collection and Analysis in Learning Technology and CCI Research

Abstract Conducting experimental studies in learning technology and CCI research entails an iterative process of observation, rationalization, and validation. Although data collection and data analysis procedures may vary widely in complexity, their selection is based on the research objectives, RQs or hypotheses. So the researchers need to carefully select them and make sure that the research design decisions of data collection and analysis, are adequate for the goals of the study. This chapter provides information on the various data collections and analyses that are usually employed in learning technology and CCI research. This chapter is intended to serve as a guide for CCI and learning technology researchers, and help them deciding what data they need to collect and how they should analyze them to address the goals of their study.

Keywords Learning technology · Child-computer interaction · Data collection · Data analysis

As mentioned in the introduction, conducting experimental studies in learning technology and CCI research entails an iterative process of observation, rationalization, and validation (see Fig. 6.1). More detailed processes with additional steps, such as conducting a literature review, have been proposed (e.g., Ross & Morrison, 2013). Nevertheless, no matter how detailed description we have, determining, conducting, and reporting the data analysis is fundamental. Although data analysis procedures vary widely in complexity, selection of the appropriate analysis is usually based on two aspects: the RQs/hypotheses and the type of data involved. To clarify the process, Fig. 6.1 shows the steps typically needed to determine the process and conduct the data analysis.

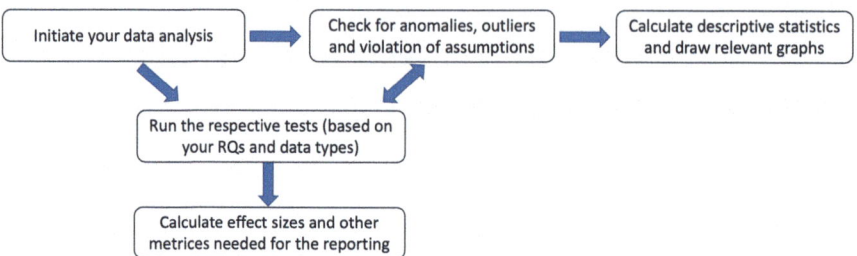

Fig. 6.1 Typical process for determining and conducting data analysis in learning technology and CCI studies

6.1 Data Collection

There are different ways that researchers collect data. Whether it is qualitative, quantitative or mixed research design, researchers need to collect data that are going to support the rationalization of the study (e.g., respond to the hypotheses or the RQs). In particular, in human-factors IT-related fields, we usually see different quantitative (e.g., log files/analytics, questionnaire data, sensor data) or/and qualitative (e.g., interviews, field notes) data collections taking place. Although it is possible to follow some of the principles described in this section with qualitative data as well, through different forms of data quantification (e.g., annotations, text mining, expert analysis); most of the practices described here concern quantitative data collections. In several cases those data collections are associated with specific measurements (which are associated with the RQs), in some data collections the measurements are predefined (e.g., questionnaire data, some log files) in some other data collections the measurements are post-computed (e.g., from sensor data), and in some other data collections there are no measurements (e.g., this is common in qualitative research studies). In this section, we will see some example data collections that are relevant for a learning technology and CCI researcher.

Questionnaire Data (Also Known as Survey Data) The use of questionnaires (also called surveys) has a long history in both HCI and learning technology research. The goal is to understand users/learners attitudes and perceptions toward an artifact, or/and a procedure. Questionnaires are also allowing us to gather information about users' backgrounds (e.g., habits, technology use), demographics and awareness. Questionnaires have been used for several years across different fields, such as social psychology, behavioral research and marketing, and can be put into practice in a pen and paper form or as a part of the system (e.g., integrated questionnaires). Several standardized questionnaires have been developed to gather information about system's perceived usability (e.g., System Usability Scale (SUS) (Brooke, 1996), Computer System Usability Questionnaires (CSUQ) (Lewis, 1995)), users' perceived effort (e.g., NASA Task Load Index (NASA-TLX) (Hart & Staveland, 1988)), and users' attitudes and perceptions (e.g., perceived usefulness, perceived ease of use (Davis, 1989). Questionnaires are a direct means of measuring users' perceived experience such as satisfaction, enjoyment, ease of use, with many of them having high level of standardization in HCI research (e.g., satisfaction is part of the ISO 9241). In the same vein, questionnaires are systematically used to assess learning experience, several questionnaire instruments have been developed and widely used in the past (e.g., to evaluate a learning system or different aspects of the learning design) (see: Kay & Knaack, 2009; Henrie et al., 2015). Questionnaires is a commonly accepted measure of users' and learners' experience (at least the perceived one), and despite some criticism (e.g., overuse or overreliance on questionnaires), questionnaires will probably continue to be a valid approach for externalizing and quantifying users' perceived experience. Below in Fig. 6.2 you can see two standard questionnaires for measuring system's usability (left) and users' mental effort (right).

In this book we are not going to have a deep discussion on the role of questionnaires in IT related research, such a discussion can be found in Müller et al. (2014) and Groves et al. (2011). However, we will briefly discuss how questionnaires can help us collecting useful data and what are the most common measurements we see in learning technology and HCI research. The most common conceptual constructs (measurements) are multi item (multi questions), so several similar question are used to construct the measurement of the construct. In most of the cases, they are measured using Likert scales (e.g., five or seven point are the most common) and the wording of the scales can be configured to match the question.[1] Although no strict requirements exist, in large scale studies (usually survey studies) we see expectations for ten respondents per item (question). In experimental designs we see studies with less respondents per item. However, the researchers need to be considerable of the "ecology" of the measurements (e.g., should have a manageable number of questions that allow the user to understand, reflect and respond). Beyond the care the researchers need to pay during the research design of a study, there are also procedures for assessing the convergent validity of questionnaire measurements used in a study, for instance Fornell and Larcker (1981) proposed the following three routines, composite reliability of each measurement, usually Cronbach α above 0.7; item/question reliability of the measure, usually factor loading of 0.7 and above for each question (with no cross loadings) is a good indicator; and the Average Variance Extracted (AVE) of the measure, usually it is expected that AVE is equal or exceeds 0.50. In the following table (Table 6.1) we provide some examples of commonly used (in learning technology and HCI) measurements. Those items are properly contextualized and provided as options to a general question such as "Please indicate how much you agree or disagree with the following statements based on your experience with [the artifact]:". Whenever [the artifact] the researchers can use the artifact of interest (e.g., the XYZ mobile application, the avatar, the dashboard).

---

[1] Examples of Likert Scaled Responses Used in Data-Gathering: https://mwcc.edu/wp-content/uploads/2020/09/Likert-Scale-Response-Options_MWCC.pdf

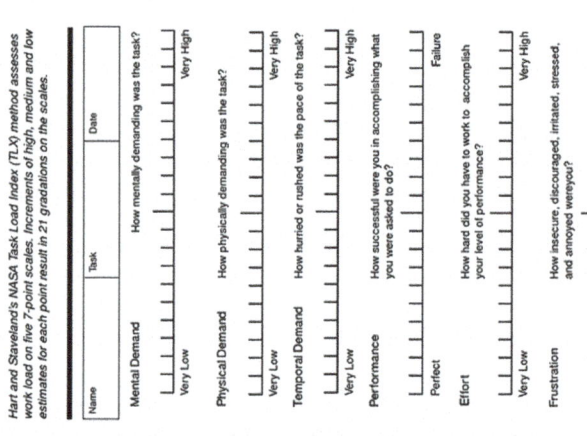

Graded SUS questionnaire demonstrating how the score for each of item of the SUS is determined with odd questions scored 0–4 based on the 1–5 selection, and even questions scored 4–0 based on the 1–5 selection.

The total score for this example is 26. Multiplying 26 * 2.5 gives us a SUS score of 65. From a meta-analysis studies we know that 68 is the average and your system needs to score above 80 to be on the top 10% of scores. This is also the point where users are more likely to be recommending it to a friend.

The interpretation of NASA TLX score: 0-9 (low); 10-29 (medium), 30-49 (somewhat high); 50-79 (high); 80-100 (very high).

Fig. 6.2 Standard questionnaires for measuring: system's usability (SUS; Brooke, 1996) (left). (Image from Klug, 2017; licensed under CC BY-ND 3.0).; mental effort in a task (NASA-TLX; Hart & Staveland, 1988) (right). (Image by https://commons.wikimedia.org/wiki/File:NasaTLX.png)

6.1 Data Collection

Table 6.1 Examples of measurements, their description, their questions and the respective reference

Measurement	Description	Questions (items)	References
Perceived usefulness (PU)	PU refers to the degree to which a person believes that using [this artifact] is useful for them.	Using [the artifact] improves my [learning] performance.	Davis (1989)
		Using [the artifact] enables me to accomplish my [learning] tasks more quickly.	
		Using [the artifact] makes my [learning] more productive.	
		I find [the artifact] useful for me [to learn].	
Perceived ease of use (PEOU)	PEOU refers to the degree to which a person believes that using [this artifact] will be free of effort.	Overall, [the artifact] is easy to use.	Davis (1989)
		Learning how to use [the artifact] is easy for me.	
		My interaction with [the artifact] is clear and understandable.	
		It is easy for me to [learn] through [the artifact].	
Enjoyment (ENJ)/ intrinsic motivation	ENJ refers to the degree to which a person believes that using [this artifact] is perceived to be personally enjoyable.	I find [the artifact] to be enjoyable.	Venkatesh et al. (2002)
		The actual process of using [the artifact] is pleasant.	
		I have fun using [the artifact].	
Behavioral intention (BI)	BI refers to the degree to which a person has formulated conscious plans regarding whether to perform a specified future behavior.	Assuming I had access to [the artifact], I intend to use it.	Venkatesh et al. (2002)
		Given that I had access to [the artifact], I predict that I would use it.	
[Technological] self-efficacy (SEF)	SEF refers to the self-assessment of individual ability to use [the artifact] to complete specified tasks.	I could complete my [learning] activity using [the artifact] if I had never used a system like it before.	Compeau and Higgins (1995)
		I could complete my [learning] activity using [the artifact] if I had only the system manuals for reference	
		I could complete my [learning] activity using [the artifact] if I had seen someone else using it before trying it myself.	

(continued)

Table 6.1 (continued)

Measurement	Description	Questions (items)	References
Satisfaction (SAT)	SAT refers to the degree to which a person feels positively about [the artifact].	I am satisfied with the performance of [the artifact].	Roca et al. (2006)
		I am pleased with the experience of using [the artifact].	
		My decision to use the [the artifact] was a wise one.	
Fun-Delight dimension (FUN)	FUN refers to the degree to which a person experiences the sense of fun about an activity or [an artifact].	During the activity with [the artifact], I had fun	Tisza and Markopoulos (2021)
		I want to [use] something like this again.	
		During the activity with [the artifact], I was happy.	

Analytics (Also Known as User Logs) In the fourth chapter we discussed about user traces that are left behind when users interact with technologies, and the implications those traces have for learning technology and CCI research. Those traces produce a wide range of insights, including users' response time, response correctness, number of attempts to solve a problem, time spent interacting with learning resources, navigation to various learning resources, activity on the various communication functionalities (e.g., forums), and other learning trace data. Besides the ways systems' can develop intelligence when leveraging on these data, such data can also be used to enrich measurements when conducting experimental studies. As we discussed in the fourth chapter tracking logs are powerful (you can see examples from edX MOOCs here[2]) and can help us to infer useful measurements, see services that host and provide access to learning interaction data such as Pittsburgh Science of Learning Center's DataShop (https://pslcdatashop.web.cmu.edu/). Although a perfect one-to-one relationship between "measurements" and "conceptual constructs" is practically impossible, we see that very close relationships (i.e., analytics that capture the target construct to a great extent) exist and are heavily used to CCI and learning technology research (e.g., learning performance that is defined as the scores of the user in the assessment tasks). This allows us to capture those useful measurements intuitively (e.g., via the log files). Although such measurements can be post-computed from the tracking logs of the technology and the respective database schema; it is also possible and significantly more practical to "architect" analytics when designing and developing the technology. By architecting the analytics, you can develop relational database schemas that organize the data with respect to your needs and meaningful measurements (e.g., see Pardos et al., 2016), architecting analytics is also powerful when you have to work with learning eco-systems, where analytics across systems need to be captured and make sense (Mangaroska et al., 2021). The use of analytics in measurements during experimentation is an

---

[2] EdX guide: https://edx.readthedocs.io/projects/devdata/en/stable/internal_data_formats/tracking_logs.html

6.1 Data Collection

interesting and complex topic. The goal of this book, is not to go deep in this topic, but provide some examples of commonly used analytics based measurements in the context of learning technology and CCI (see Table 6.2). These selection of those measurements needs to take into consideration the context of the study of the technology and be relevant with the intended RQ.

Table 6.2 Examples of analytics-based measurements, their description, how they are usually computed and an example of their use from the literature

Measurement	Description	Computed	Example References
Tasks accessed	How many tasks/resources have been accessed.	# of tasks/resources opened.	Heffernan and Heffernan (2014)
# of times a task/resource has been accessed	How many times a task/resource has been accessed.	# of times a task/resource has been opened.	Barthakur et al. (2021), Pardos et al. (2016)
Total time to respond	Time a learn spent to respond to a task (e.g., multiple choice question).	The timestamp created when opening the task minus the timestamp created when closing it.	Heffernan and Heffernan (2014), Papamitsiou et al. (2018)
Performance on tasks / correctness (sometimes used as a proxy for students' mastery level)	Learners' performance based on tasks' correctness (e.g., multiple choice or matching questions).	# of times tasks responded correctly (can also use a ratio of correct and incorrect responses)	Papamitsiou et al. (2018), Zamecnik et al. (2022)
Time spent	Time spent with a resource (e.g., watching a video, reading an HTML document).	Aggregated # of ms spent on a particular resource.	Barthakur et al. (2021)
Use of a functionality (e.g., hint)	The # of times a learner used a specific functionality (resource).	Aggregated # of times a resource was accessed.	Barthakur et al. (2021), Heffernan and Heffernan (2014)
Video lecture viewing activity	Viewing activity of a video resource (e.g., what segments of the video were viewed, skipped, reviewed and so on).	Modelling of students' video navigation interactions.	Giannakos et al. (2015)
# of messages posted	How many messages a student posted in a discussion media (e.g., forum).	# of messages posted by a student	Kovanović et al. (2015)
Discussion reading time	Total time spent on viewing course's online discussions.	Aggregated # of ms spent on the discussion space (e.g., forum).	Kovanović et al. (2015)
Background information	Previous courses taken, performance or other background information.	Students' learning record.	Zamecnik et al. (2022)

Sensor-Based Analytics (Sensor Data) Advances in sensors, social signal processing and computational analyses have demonstrated the potential to help us understand user and learning processes which were either not-possible to be captured or "too complex" for traditional analytics. For example, psychomotor learning with physical objects needs high frequency data and analyses can now happen in a reasonable time-window (Sharma & Giannakos, 2020). Due to the need for combining different expertise (e.g., learning scientists, data scientists, computer scientists), the collection, analysis and interpretation of sensor data in CCI and learning contexts have been a challenging endeavor. Nevertheless, over the last years the Multimodal Learning Analytics (MMLA) research community has managed to gather diverse research expertise's (e.g., educational, computational, psychological), and contributed with rich measurements with respect to HCI and learning. A perfect one-to-one relationship between sensor-based measures and conceptual constructs does not exist (Giannakos et al., 2022), however, MMLA research is achieving acceptable levels of reliability and validity, allowing us to use measurements that provide useful insights (e.g., from eye-activity, facial expression or users' motions and gestures). Table 6.3 depicts some examples of commonly used sensor based measurements in the context of learning technology and CCI. Once again, the selection of those measurements needs to take into consideration the context of the study of the technology and be relevant with the intended RQ, moreover, the researchers also need to consider the level of intrusiveness (the extent to which a measurement is ecologically valid, e.g., does not interfere with the task or impose obtrusive conditions). In different sub-domains of learning technology and HCI, we see researchers coining measurements that align with the objectives of those sub-domains. For example, in the context of Computer Supported Collaborative Learning (CSCL) research, we find researchers using a measurement called Joint Visual Attention (JVA) (i.e., the moments more than one users look at the same area) or "with-me-ness" (i.e., the moments the learner is looking on the content delivered by the teacher, e.g., how much the learner follows the teacher), although those measurements are not as general or widely used as the ones we identify in Table 6.3, they are very important for the challenges of this particular sub-domain (Sharma et al., 2014, 2017).

Pictorial Self-Report Data Traditional verbal questionnaires assume that respondents are able fully grasp a question and think abstractly about their experience. However, several populations (e.g., children younger than 12) have not yet developed these skills or are in conditions that do not allow them to respond those instruments in a valid manner (e.g., a user who has dyslexia or is very tired from the main task); instead, their thinking processes are based on mental representations that relate to concrete events, objects, or experiences. This must be taken into account when adapting the measurement method to meet participants' needs. Following this line of reasoning and related work in child development and psychology (Harter & Pike, 1984), there is an number of instruments that use visual methods (or observations and qualitative, checklist-based measurements), which we know are more

6.1 Data Collection

Table 6.3 Examples of sensor-based measurements, their description, how they are usually computed and an example of their use from the literature

Measurement	Sensing device	Description	Computed	References
Stress	Wristband	The state of being overwhelmed or unable to cope with mental or emotional pressure.	Stress is computed as temperature's decreasing slope[a]. The more negative the slope of the temperature is in a given time window, the higher the stress is.	Herborn et al. (2015); A use case: Lee-Cultura et al. (2020)
Cognitive load	Eye-tracking	The load that performing a task imposes on the cognitive system of a user.	Index of pupilary activity computed as discrete wavelet transform of the pupil diameter.	Duchowski et al. (2018); A use case: Mangaroska et al. (2022)
Interaction time with an object	Eye-tracking	Proportion of time looking at an object.	Fixation duration in an object (defined within an area of interest – AOI), an object can be the whole screen or a specific part of the screen/interface.	Giannakos et al. (2020)
Attention	Eye-tracking	On-task visual focus allocation.	Average fixation duration.	Giannakos et al. (2020)
Happiness	Facial camera	Emotions as expressed by human facial movements and extracted from the face images based on the facial action units (AUs) and OpenFace framework.	Happy (AU6, A10); Sad (AU1, AU4, AU15); Surprise (AU1, AU2, AU5, AU26); Anger (AU4, AU5, AU7, AU23).	AUs: Ekman et al. (2002); OpenFace framework: Amos et al. (2016); A use case: Lee-Cultura et al. (2020)
Sadness	Facial camera			
Anger	Facial camera			
Surprise	Facial camera			
Movement	Motion sensing input device (e.g., Kinect)	The total distance travelled by the user.	The total distance travelled by each joint in the skeleton data, averaged over the whole body.	Lee-Cultura et al. (2020)

[a]Stress can also be measured by combining measurements (e.g., temperature, heart rate, galvanic skin response), see: Basjaruddin et al. (2021)

effective than verbal methods (Döring et al., 2010). Such visual analogs represent specific situations, behaviors, and people to whom a user can easily relate.

Such visual analogs are usually employed to collect data during evaluation of an artefact (as well as during the lifetime of an application). We have seen pictorial questionnaires popping up while we are using an application or at the end of an activity (e.g., after we try a resource that has been recommended to us). Similarly with the verbal questionnaires, pictorial questionnaires are used to qualtify users' perceived experience such as satisfaction, enjoyment, ease of use and alike. Although pictorial questionnaires usually do not follow the multi item (multi question) paradigm of the verbal ones (so the validity is not always being assessed), however, it is easier to employ pictorial questionnaires "on the spot" and capture temporal experience of the users. Moreover due to their usually short reading time, it is also easy to employ them either in selected critical moments (when the user finished a task) or in a random manner during the activity so we can get repeated measurements (Fig. 6.3).

Pictorial questionnaires are not meant to substitute verbal questionnaires, those two types of self-reporting instruments have been designed to address different research needs. Verbal questionnaires can use the specificity of verbal communication to extract exact information and the widely used measurements have been extensively validated and standardized. Pictorial questionnaires are used when "verbal communication becomes a challenge" and have the benefits of not increasing users' cognitive load and overall burden, and reducing the time-to-complete. Similarly with verbal questionnaires, the pictorial questionnaires should be properly contextualized and sometimes complemented with minimal text such as "what do you think about [the artifact]:". Whenever [the artifact] the researchers can use the artifact of interest (e.g., the XYZ mobile application, the avatar, the dashboard). Nevertheless, pictorial questionnaires should be self-standing, even if the user cannot read the provided text, depending the end-user, sometimes researchers need to use oral communication to explain what aspects we are asking the end-user to rate with the visual analogs. Similarly with verbal questionnaires, pictorial questionnaires can be used in both pen and paper and in a digital version, however, some of the advantages of digitally administering pictorial questionnaires to assess software (e.g., temporality, overall burden) might be lost or weakened. Table 6.4 depicts

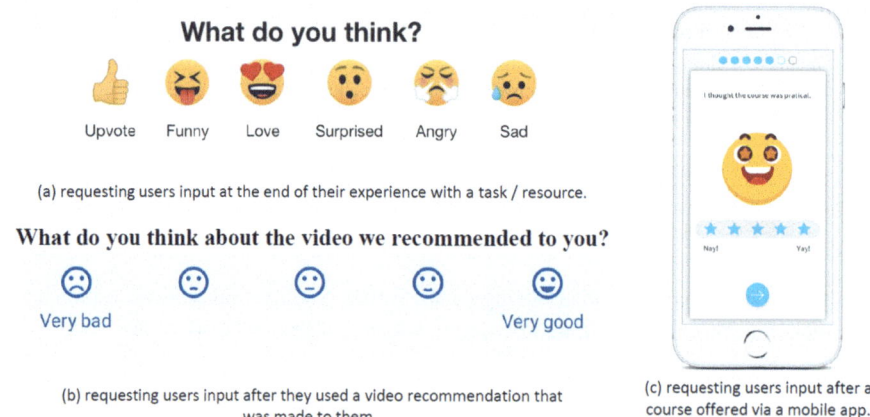

Fig. 6.3 Three examples of pictorial surveys used to evaluate users' experience

6.1 Data Collection

Table 6.4 Examples of pictorial survey measurements, their description, how they look like and the respective reference

Measurement	Description	Exemplar	References
The self-assessment manikin (SAM)[a]	SAM a pictorial scale for the measurement of pleasure, arousal, and dominance, it is one of the most popular visual self-reporting tools.	Valence (top), arousal (middle), dominance (bottom) with permission by Elsevier. Valence (top), arousal (middle), dominance (bottom) with permission by Elsevier.	Bradley and Lang (1994)
Sorémo – Emotional states	Sorémo was developed with the goal to measure children's emotional states while children use educational software.	licensed under CC BY-ND 4.0	Girard (2011)
Smileyometers – Assessment of fun	Smileyometers[b] is used to measure users' fun, it is designed to support children's assessment of an application of a product.	Awful Not very good Good Really good Brilliant — with permission by ACM	Read and MacFarlane (2006)

(continued)

Table 6.4 (continued)

Measurement	Description	Exemplar	References
The AffectButton	The AffectButton is an interface component (a medium-sized) button that presents one dynamically changing iconic facial expression which changes based on the coordinates of the user's pointer in the button. The user selects the most appropriate expression by clicking the button.	The AffectButton in a simple window (left), its extreme affective states (right), and four example trajectories from neutral to extreme PAD states with corresponding mouse pointer location (down), with permission by Elsevier.	Broekens and Brinkman (2013)
Pictorial system usability scale (P-SUS)	PSUS is a multi-item scale aiming to measure the perceived usability of mobile devices. The scale is based on the established verbal SUS.	Three (out of the ten) items of the P-SUS, licensed under CC BY-ND 4.0	Baumgartne et al. (2019)

6.1 Data Collection

Pick-A-mood	Pick-A-mood is a cartoon-based scale that enables the measurement of eight distinct mood types, and can be used in both qualitative and quantitative research settings.	Pick-A-mood female character (different characters can be selected) expressing nine mood states (Left: Neutral; top left to right: Calm, relaxed, cheerful, excited; bottom left to right: Sad, bored, tense, irritated). Licensed under CC BY-ND 3.0	Desmet et al. (2016)

[a]SAM is widely used and validated, but in the context of CCI, children have difficulties understanding the SAM (e.g., often misunderstand the depicted emotions)

[b]By using it in a pre-post manner, the child can give a score for the expected (pre) and the experienced (post) fun. Comparing these two scores allows you to see if children have had a good experience (more info in the CCI UX Playbook: https://chici.org/ux-playbook/)

some examples of commonly used pictorial questionnaire measurements in the context of learning technology and CCI.

6.2 Data Analysis

To make the process clearer and to provide additional resources, Table 6.5 summarizes the most common data analysis procedures used in learning technology and CCI research. Let us now think of a simple between-subjects design with one control group (e.g., no use of dashboard in the LMS) and one experimental group (e.g., a simple dashboard that provides students' previous test scores), with students' weekly test scores as the dependent variable. In this case, a t-test for independent samples is needed (provided that parametric assumptions are met) to test the hypothesis that introducing a simple dashboard affects students' learning performance. Adding a second experimental group (i.e., a third treatment group) with a dashboard that not only provides but also visualizes students' scores will require a different analysis. In that case, we will need a one-way analysis of variance (ANOVA) (provided that parametric assumptions are met) to compare the three means; if the results of the ANOVA are significant, we can conduct a follow-up Tukey or REGWQ post-hoc comparison of means to find the pairwise differences. Learning technology and CCI researchers do not have to be data analysts or statisticians, but it is important to provide clear RQs and hypotheses and to follow a few basic rules and guidelines during the data analysis. Clearly formulated RQs will also make it possible to work with data analysts or statisticians if more sophisticated analyses are required that go beyond the scope of this book.

Most of the studies in learning technology and CCI employ the null hypothesis significance testing (NHST)[3] approaches and analyse data using the variance-based methods we present in Table 6.5. Despite the usefulness of variance-based approaches we have seen an increasing the need for new methods as well as combinations of different methods and approaches that can reduce biases and help us obtain a more holistic understanding of the phenomenon. Examples of such methods that we see being increasingly used in HCI and learning technology/ analytics are Bayesian methods (Robertson & Kaptein, 2016), fuzzy-set qualitative comparative analysis (fsQCA, or simpler versions of it such as QCA) (Pappas et al., 2019; Papamitsiou et al., 2018), process mining (Sharma et al., forthcoming), Hidden Markov Models (Sharma et al., 2020), or different machine learning methods (Kidziński et al., 2016).

As mentioned above, to support learning technology/CCI researchers, we provide a comprehensive how-to guide that allows them to choose between the various analyses by looking at the data types, the function of each of the analyses, working examples, the main conditions and assumptions, and resources for step-by-step

---

[3] NHST is statistical inference by which an experimental factor is tested against a hypothesis.

6.1 Data Collection

Table 6.5 Comparison of data analysis procedures in learning technology and CCI research

Data type	Function	Example	Assumptions met?[a]	Type of analysis	Does it test causal effects?	Open resources[b] (Based on Field, 2018, for IBM SPSS software)
Any	Describes different measurements in different groups	What is the average student learning performance score (LPS) of students who used the dashboard?	N/A	Calculation (and often visualization) of different descriptive measures, which can be of four types: **frequency** (e.g., count, percent, frequency), **central tendency** (e.g., mean, median, mode), **dispersion or variation** (e.g., range, variance, standard deviation), and **position** (e.g., percentile ranks, quartile ranks)	No	Descriptive stats and graph capabilities: https://www.discoveringstatistics.com/repository/revisespss.pdf
		What is the percentage of students who completed task Y?				Editing graphs: https://youtu.be/en0t0QS9uo8
Ind. var. = categorical **Dep. var. = categorical**	Tests the **relationship/independence between two categorical (variables)**	Is school district (A vs. B) related to passing college entry tests (pass vs. no-pass)?	N/A	Chi-square test of independence	No	Handout and video: https://www.discoveringstatistics.com/statistics-hell-p/egestes-predicting-categorical-outcomes/chi-square-test/
Ind. var. = continuous **Dep. var. = continuous**	Tests the **relationship between two variables**	Is stress related to LPS?	Yes	Pearson correlation (Pearson's r)	No	Correlations handout: https://www.discoveringstatistics.com/repository/correlation_spss.pdf
Ind. var. = continuous **Dep. var. = continuous**	Tests the **relationship between two variables**	Is attention related to learning performance scores?	No	Spearman correlation (Spearman's ρ) or Kendall correlation (Kendall's τ)	No	Correlations video tutorial: https://youtu.be/ltOSxnNc3Tg

(continued)

Table 6.5 (continued)

Data type	Function	Example	Assumptions met?[a]	Type of analysis	Does it test causal effects?	Open resources[b] (Based on Field, 2018, for IBM SPSS software)
Ind. var. = categorical Dep. **var. = continuous**	Tests the **differences between two groups**	Does the dashboard group have better LPS than the non-dashboard group?	Yes	Independent t-test	Yes	Handout: https://www.discoveringstatistics.com/repository/t_test.pdf Video tutorial: https://www.youtube.com/watch?v=EkbkI7x6bNA
Ind. var. = categorical Dep. **var. = continuous**	Tests the **differences between two groups**	Does the dashboard group have better LPS than the non-dashboard group?	No	Bootstrapped t-test or Mann–Whitney U test	Yes	Mann–Whitney handout: https://www.discoveringstatistics.com/repository/nonparametric.pdf Video: https://www.youtube.com/watch?v=esNb6RFIXvw

6.1 Data Collection

Ind. var. = categorical **Dep. var.** = continuous	Tests the **differences between three (or more) groups**	Will there be differences in LPS among the three groups (non-dashboard, dashboard, and adaptive dashboard)?	Yes	Analysis of variance (ANOVA); if significant, follow-up with Tukey or REGWQ post-hoc comparison of means	Yes	Handout: https://www.discoveringstatistics.com/repository/onewayanova.pdf Video tutorial: https://www.youtube.com/watch?v=ehOWuOcyejI
Ind. var. = categorical **Dep. var.** = continuous	Tests the **differences between three (or more) groups**	Will there be differences in the LPS among the three groups (non-dashboard, dashboard, and adaptive dashboard)?	No	Robust ANOVA or Kruskal–Wallis test; if significant, follow-up with games–Howell post-hoc comparison of mean	Yes	
Ind. var. = categorical **Dep. var.** = continuous	Tests the **difference between two treatment means for a given group**	Will students change their opinion about the use of dashboards after the use of a dashboard (based on a pre-post test)?	Yes	Paired-sample t-test (dependent t-test)	Yes	Handout: https://www.discoveringstatistics.com/repository/t_test.pdf Video tutorial: https://www.youtube.com/watch?v=Ekbkl7x6bNA

(continued)

Table 6.5 (continued)

Data type	Function	Example	Assumptions met?[a]	Type of analysis	Does it test causal effects?	Open resources[b] (Based on Field, 2018, for IBM SPSS software)
Ind. var. = categorical **Dep. var. = continuous**	Tests the **difference between two treatment means for a given group**	Will students' change their opinion about the use of dashboards after the use of a dashboard (based on a pre-post test)?	No	Bootstrapped t-test or Wilcoxon signed-rank test	Yes	Wilcoxon handout: https://www.discoveringstatistics.com/repository/nonparametric.pdf Video tutorial: https://www.youtube.com/watch?v=dkobjvhxTro
Ind. var. = categorical **Dep. var. = continuous**	Tests the difference between two (or more) treatment means on two or more dependent variables (by controlling type I error rate across the measure)	Will there be differences in the LPS and students' attitudes among the three groups (non-dashboard, dashboard, and adaptive dashboard)?	Yes	Multivariate analysis of variance (MANOVA); if significant, follow-up with ANOVA on each individual measure	Yes	MANOVA video tutorial: https://www.youtube.com/watch?v=m0zV_wFGA1I&t=1s

[a]Parametric assumptions are linearity (the relationship between X and the mean of Y is linear), homoscedasticity (the variance of the residual is the same for any value of X), independence (observations are independent of each other), and normality (for any fixed value of X, Y is normally distributed)
[b]The resources provided are for IBM SPSS statistics software, but similar resources are available for R (e.g., Field et al., 2012), Python (e.g., Haslwanter, 2016), and other statistical analysis software. The statistical language/tool used does not affect the information provided in this table or the outcome and reporting of the analyses

implementation. Novice researchers should be aware that in order to explore causal relationships (cause-and-effect relationships) on the basis of experimental designs that compare outcomes associated with treatments, it is necessary to use tests that test causal effects (e.g., t-tests or ANOVAs) rather than correlational tests (e.g., Pearson correlations).

References

Amos, B., Ludwiczuk, B., & Satyanarayanan, M. (2016). Openface: A general-purpose face recognition library with mobile applications. *CMU School of Computer Science, 6*(2), 20.

Barthakur, A., Kovanovic, V., Joksimovic, S., Siemens, G., Richey, M., & Dawson, S. (2021). Assessing program-level learning strategies in MOOCs. *Computers in Human Behavior, 117*, 106674.

Basjaruddin, N. C., Syahbarudin, F., & Sutjiredjeki, E. (2021). Measurement device for stress level and vital sign based on sensor fusion. *Healthcare Informatics Research, 27*(1), 11–18.

Baumgartner, J., Frei, N., Kleinke, M., Sauer, J., & Sonderegger, A. (2019, May). Pictorial system usability scale (P-SUS) developing an instrument for measuring perceived usability. In *Proceedings of the 2019 chi conference on human factors in computing systems* (pp. 1–11).

Bradley, M. M., & Lang, P. J. (1994). Measuring emotion: The self-assessment manikin and the semantic differential. *Journal of Behavior Therapy and Experimental Psychiatry, 25*(1), 49–59.

Broekens, J., & Brinkman, W. P. (2013). AffectButton: A method for reliable and valid affective self-report. *International Journal of Human-Computer Studies, 71*(6), 641–667.

Brooke, J. (1996). SUS-A quick and dirty usability scale. *Usability Evaluation in Industry, 189*, 194.

Compeau, D. R., & Higgins, C. A. (1995). Computer self-efficacy: Development of a measure and initial test. *MIS Quarterly*, 189–211.

Davis, F. D. (1989). Perceived usefulness, perceived ease of use, and user acceptance of information technology. *MIS Quarterly, 13*(3), 319–340.

Desmet, P. M. A., Vastenburg, M. H., & Romero, N. (2016). *Pick-A-Mood manual: Pictorial self-report scale for measuring mood states*. Delft University of Technology.

Döring, A. K., Blauensteiner, A., Aryus, K., Drögekamp, L., & Bilsky, W. (2010). Assessing values at an early age: The picture-based value survey for children. *Journal of Personality Assessment, 92*, 439–448. https://doi.org/10.1080/00223891.2010.497423

Duchowski, A. T., Krejtz, K., Krejtz, I., Biele, C., Niedzielska, A., Kiefer, P., … & Giannopoulos, I. (2018). The index of pupillary activity: Measuring cognitive load vis-à-vis task difficulty with pupil oscillation. In *Proceedings of the 2018 CHI conference on human factors in computing systems* (pp. 1–13).

Ekman, P., Friesen, W. V., & Hager, J. C. (2002). *Facial action coding system: Facial action coding system: The manual: On CD-ROM*. Research Nexus.

Field, A. (2018). *Discovering statistics using IBM SPSS statistics* (5th ed.). Sage.

Field, A., Miles, J., & Field, Z. (2012). *Discovering statistics using R*. Sage.

Fornell, C., & Larcker, D. F. (1981). Evaluating structural equation models with unobservable variables and measurement error. *Journal of Marketing Research, 18*(1), 39–50.

Giannakos, M. N., Chorianopoulos, K., & Chrisochoides, N. (2015). Making sense of video analytics: Lessons learned from clickstream interactions, attitudes, and learning outcome in a video-assisted course. *The International Review of Research in Open and Distance Learning, 16*(1), 260–283.

Giannakos, M. N., Papavlasopoulou, S., & Sharma, K. (2020). Monitoring children's learning through wearable eye-tracking: The case of a making-based coding activity. *IEEE Pervasive Computing, 19*(1), 10–21.

Giannakos, M., Spikol, D., Di Mitri, D., Sharma, K., & Ochoa, X. (2022). Introduction to multimodal learning analytics. In *Multimodal learning analytics handbook*. Springer.

Girard, S. A. S. (2011). *Traffic lights and smiley faces: Do children learn mathematics better with affective open-learner modelling tutors?* (Doctoral dissertation, University of Bath).

Groves, R. M., Fowler, F. J., Jr., Couper, M. P., Lepkowski, J. M., Singer, E., & Tourangeau, R. (2011). *Survey methodology*. Wiley.

Hart, S. G., & Staveland, L. E. (1988). Development of NASA-TLX (task load index): Results of empirical and theoretical research. *Human Mental Workload, 1*, 139–183.

Harter, S., & Pike, R. (1984). The pictorial scale of perceived competence and social acceptance for young children. *Child Development, 55*, 1969–1982. https://doi.org/10.2307/1129772

Haslwanter, T. (2016). *An introduction to statistics with python. With applications in the life sciences*. Springer International Publishing.

Heffernan, N. T., & Heffernan, C. L. (2014). The ASSISTments ecosystem: Building a platform that brings scientists and teachers together for minimally invasive research on human learning and teaching. *International Journal of Artificial Intelligence in Education, 24*(4), 470–497.

Henrie, C. R., Halverson, L. R., & Graham, C. R. (2015). Measuring student engagement in technology-mediated learning: A review. *Computers & Education, 90*, 36–53.

Herborn, K. A., Graves, J. L., Jerem, P., Evans, N. P., Nager, R., McCafferty, D. J., & McKeegan, D. E. (2015). Skin temperature reveals the intensity of acute stress. *Physiology & Behavior, 152*, 225–230.

Kay, R. H., & Knaack, L. (2009). Assessing learning, quality and engagement in learning objects: The learning object evaluation scale for students (LOES-S). *Educational Technology Research and Development, 57*(2), 147–168.

Kidziński, Ł., Giannakos, M., Sampson, D. G., & Dillenbourg, P. (2016). A tutorial on machine learning in educational science. *State-of-the-Art and Future Directions of Smart Learning*, 453–459.

Klug, B. (2017). An overview of the system usability scale in library website and system usability testing. *Weave: Journal of Library User Experience, 1*(6).

Kovanović, V., Gašević, D., Joksimović, S., Hatala, M., & Adesope, O. (2015). Analytics of communities of inquiry: Effects of learning technology use on cognitive presence in asynchronous online discussions. *The Internet and Higher Education, 27*, 74–89.

Lee-Cultura, S., Sharma, K., Papavlasopoulou, S., Retalis, S., & Giannakos, M. (2020). Using sensing technologies to explain children's self-representation in motion-based educational games. In *Proceedings of the interaction design and children conference* (pp. 541–555).

Lewis, J. R. (1995). IBM computer usability satisfaction questionnaires: Psychometric evaluation and instructions for use. *International Journal of Human-Computer Interaction, 7*(1), 57–78.

Mangaroska, K., Vesin, B., Kostakos, V., Brusilovsky, P., & Giannakos, M. N. (2021). Architecting analytics across multiple E-learning systems to enhance learning design. *IEEE Transactions on Learning Technologies, 14*(2), 173–188.

Mangaroska, K., Sharma, K., Gašević, D., & Giannakos, M. (2022). Exploring students' cognitive and affective states during problem solving through multimodal data: Lessons learned from a programming activity. *Journal of Computer Assisted Learning, 38*(1), 40–59.

Müller, H., Sedley, A., & Ferrall-Nunge, E. (2014). Survey research in HCI. In *Ways of knowing in HCI* (pp. 229–266). Springer.

Papamitsiou, Z., Economides, A. A., Pappas, I. O., & Giannakos, M. N. (2018). Explaining learning performance using response-time, self-regulation and satisfaction from content: an fsQCA approach. In *Proceedings of the 8th international conference on learning analytics and knowledge* (pp. 181–190).

Pappas, I. O., Giannakos, M. N., & Sampson, D. G. (2019). Fuzzy set analysis as a means to understand users of 21st-century learning systems: The case of mobile learning and reflections on learning analytics research. *Computers in Human Behavior, 92*, 646–659.

References

Pardos, Z. A., Whyte, A., & Kao, K. (2016). moocRP: Enabling open learning analytics with an open source platform for data distribution, analysis, and visualization. *Technology, Knowledge and Learning, 21*(1), 75–98.

Read, J. C., & MacFarlane, S. (2006). Using the fun toolkit and other survey methods to gather opinions in child computer interaction. In *Proceedings of the 2006 conference on Interaction design and children* (pp. 81–88).

Robertson, J., & Kaptein, M. (Eds.). (2016). *Modern statistical methods for HCI*. Springer.

Roca, J. C., Chiu, C. M., & Martínez, F. J. (2006). Understanding e-learning continuance intention: An extension of the technology acceptance model. *International Journal of Human-Computer Studies, 64*(8), 683–696.

Ross, S. M., & Morrison, G. R. (2013). Experimental research methods. In *Handbook of research on educational communications and technology* (pp. 1007–1029). Routledge.

Sharma, K., & Giannakos, M. (2020). Multimodal data capabilities for learning: What can multimodal data tell us about learning? *British Journal of Educational Technology, 51*(5), 1450–1484.

Sharma, K., Jermann, P., & Dillenbourg, P. (2014). "With-me-ness": A -measure for students' attention in MOOCs. In *International conference of the learning sciences* (No. EPFL-CONF-201918).

Sharma, K., Jermann, P., Dillenbourg, P., Prieto, L. P., D'Angelo, S., Gergle, D., et al. (2017). *CSCL and eye-tracking: Experiences, opportunities and challenges*. International Society of the Learning Sciences.

Sharma, K., Papamitsiou, Z., Olsen, J. K., & Giannakos, M. (2020). Predicting learners' effortful behaviour in adaptive assessment using multimodal data. In *Proceedings of the tenth international conference on learning analytics & knowledge* (pp. 480–489).

Sharma, K., Papamitsiou, Z., & Giannakos, M. (forthcoming). When is the best moment to give feedback? A pattern-based approach with multimodal data.

Tisza, G., & Markopoulos, P. (2021). FunQ: Measuring the fun experience of a learning activity with adolescents. *Current Psychology*, 1–21.

Venkatesh, V., Speier, C., & Morris, M. G. (2002). User acceptance enablers in individual decision making about technology: Toward an integrated model. *Decision Sciences, 33*(2), 297–316.

Zamecnik, A., Kovanović, V., Joksimović, S., & Liu, L. (2022). Exploring non-traditional learner motivations and characteristics in online learning: A learner profile study. *Computers and Education: Artificial Intelligence, 3*, 100051.

Open Access This chapter is licensed under the terms of the Creative Commons Attribution 4.0 International License (http://creativecommons.org/licenses/by/4.0/), which permits use, sharing, adaptation, distribution and reproduction in any medium or format, as long as you give appropriate credit to the original author(s) and the source, provide a link to the Creative Commons license and indicate if changes were made.

The images or other third party material in this chapter are included in the chapter's Creative Commons license, unless indicated otherwise in a credit line to the material. If material is not included in the chapter's Creative Commons license and your intended use is not permitted by statutory regulation or exceeds the permitted use, you will need to obtain permission directly from the copyright holder.

Chapter 7
Reporting CCI and Learning Technology Research

Abstract Designing and conducting high quality research is extremely important in CCI and learning technology research. However, the same high-quality needs to be followed during the reporting of the work. At the end of the day, this what the reviewers and readers will credit – therefore, reporting is of equal importance. This chapter provides information on how you should structure your article and the information that is usually required. This chapter is intended to serve as a template for CCI and learning technology researchers. Moreover, I have summarized some recommendations based on my experience, as well as on published guidelines and recommendations from neighboring fields.

Keywords Learning technology · Child-computer interaction · Guidelines · Reporting research

For CCI and learning technology research to be disseminated, it is important that it be efficiently reported (and published) in various proceedings, and journals. Reporting CCI and learning technology research has many similarities with other human-factors IT-related fields, such as game technology, computing education research, HCI/interaction design, and software engineering. This is due to the fact that most of these fields rely heavily on the guidelines of the American Psychological Association (APA) for reporting. The recommendations of this section are based on the authors' experience, as well as on published guidelines and recommendations from the relevant fields (e.g., Ko et al., 2015; Recker, 2012; Wobbrock, 2015; Ross & Morrison, 2013) and the APA journal article reporting standards (JARS) for reporting quantitative research (reporting the findings of a study using numeric representations),[1] qualitative research (reporting the findings of a study using narrative representations),[2] and mixed methods research (reporting the findings of a study

---

[1] Quantitative Design Reporting Standards: https://apastyle.apa.org/jars/quant-table-1.pdf
[2] Qualitative Design Reporting Standards: https://apastyle.apa.org/jars/qual-table-1.pdf

```
Title
Abstract
Keywords
    1. Introduction (and motivation)
    2. Background and related work
    3. Method (or methodologies)
        3.1. Participants
        3.2. Settings/procedure (or settings and procedure)
        3.3. Data collection (and measurements, if relevant)
        3.4. Research design
        3.5. Data analysis
    4. Findings (or results)
    5. Discussion
    6. Conclusion and future research
Contributions statement
Ethical considerations (not established yet, but becoming more and more
common)
Acknowledgments
References
```

Fig. 7.1 Typical structure for a learning technology or CCI paper/report

using both narrative and numeric representations).[3] Therefore, independently of the statistical analysis software or data science programming language you use, your reporting must follow a standard structure and include the information indicated in the conventions. Several resources are available, including the JARS website (https://apastyle.apa.org/jars), which includes details about how to report your results for a wide range of research designs and statistical analyses. There is also a summary of how to report the results of your statistical analyses provided by Dr. Jeffrey Kahn from Illinois State University (https://psychology.illinoisstate.edu/selandau/ReportingStatisticsinAPAStyle.html). This section provides a brief overview of how to report CCI and learning technology research. Figure 7.1 shows the high-level structure of a typical paper/report.

Abstract An abstract is mandatory in most reports/papers. Its purpose is to provide potential readers with an overview of the paper so that they can determine if it is relevant to their research. The abstract should be no longer than 250 words and should briefly cover each of the necessary elements (in one or two sentences per element). Effective abstracts describe three things: (1) what was done, (2) how it was done, and (3) what was found (the main results). Be specific; for instance, instead of "many" or "most," say "84%." The abstract should include the following elements. It is generally up to the writer whether to keep the words (here, in bold) that indicate the section labels.

---

[3] Mixed Methods Design Reporting Standards (in conjunction with relevant JARS–Qual and JARS–Quant guidelines): https://apastyle.apa.org/jars/mixed-table-1.pdf

- **Contribution.** Briefly describe the new knowledge emerging from the study.
- **Background.** Briefly describe the rationale for the study presented in the manuscript. The background is expected to provide a rationale for the study (i.e., why the study is needed). It is expected to establish a context that suggests the study has broad application in many programs across the world.
- **Research questions.** Briefly present the RQs that the study addresses.
- **Methodology.** Briefly describe the research methodology used to conduct the study. This section should also briefly mention limitations of the study (e.g., small sample size).
- **Findings.** Briefly summarize the findings of the study.

7.1 Introduction (and Motivation)

The introduction is used to explain the motivation of your paper to the reader. Its primary purpose is to explain why you did the work you did. In particular, the introduction needs to address five major points. Although you are also free to structure your introduction in the following way (or not), make sure you cover the five points.

The topic. This is a description of issues in whatever "world" is relevant to your topic (e.g., learning visualizations, AR/VR technology in education, or game-based learning in the classroom). This part of the introduction begins with general information about the topic and then narrows to the specific focus of the new study (normally in the last sentence of the paragraph). Definitions of key terms may also be provided. In this section, the researcher carefully selects previously published articles to establish a foundation for the study that is being reported. This helps the reader to contextualize the study's topic(s) and findings. Drawing on the popular press can be helpful in supporting your cause.

The gap. This is a description of the gap between what is known and what needs to be known. Here, challenges or problems can be framed as an opportunity, as you can motivate your work by connecting it to things that matter to people. "Absence from the literature" alone is not a good justification, although it is useful to add after you have established a problem or opportunity that is worth pursuing in its own right. As a stand-alone motivational statement, however, absence from the literature is not convincing (e.g., maybe the literature is silent on an issue because the issue is not important). Near the end of this section, you should establish a gap in the previously reported studies and identify what questions still need to be answered (e.g., by mentioning the major papers that deal with the topic, what they have accomplished, and their major flaws/omissions/neglected issues). This is an important part of the published study, because it tells the reader how your study's findings relate to and increase the knowledge base.

The goal. After describing the gap, you need to describe the goal of the study. Devoting a paragraph to the goal in the introduction is reasonable, as it allows you to describe the research or inquiry question(s) of the study. Sometimes the inquiry question or statement will be in its own section, and sometimes it will form part of the introduction. Either way, this paragraph of the introduction should provide some description of the goal and the respective research objectives/RQs. It should clarify how the proposed research objectives/RQs address the previously identified flaws/omissions/neglected issues and why it is important to address them (not every omission is important, and some issues may not have been addressed because they are trivial).

What you did and what you found. After clarifying the goal, you need to describe what the study does (in more detail than in the abstract) and offer some key results. It is important to describe what the study does through the lens of the aforementioned goal (showing that you have adopted the optimal approach for addressing your goal). In addition, it is important to give a brief overview of the major findings.

How this study contributes. A good way to end your introduction is by framing the contributions that your work makes. The contribution can be structured as a bulleted or numbered list within a paragraph. Most papers will make two to three contributions. Overstating your contribution can lead to criticism from reviewers, and even to the rejection of the paper; therefore, whatever expectations and research claims you make in the introduction must be delivered in the rest of the paper and discussed thoroughly in the discussion section. Therefore, it is important to be as clear as possible.

By structuring your introduction around these five major points (one paragraph per point; a maximum of two paragraphs if a particular point needs further elaboration), you succinctly motivate the work in relation to a real problem or opportunity, and you hook the reader with the key results and contributions. Reviewers' opinions about the importance and quality of a work are formed while reading the introduction. If it reads poorly or is missing key aspects (i.e., if it fails several of the tests implicit in the structure above, such as importance of the topic, a clear gap, concrete research objectives, and specific contributions), reviewers' opinions can very quickly tilt negatively. Examples of introduction and motivation sections that follow this clean structure can be found here, one in the context of avatars in motion-based educational games (Lee-Cultura et al., 2020), and one in the context of wearable devices for estimating the learning experience (Giannakos et al., 2020).

7.2 Background and Related Work

The primary function of the background and related work section is to answer the following four questions: What are the major/important relevant works in this topical area? What did they do? What did they find? How is this work here different (e.g., in terms of extending or complementing previous work)? This section may also include relevant theories and be called "Related work and background theories" (or similar). The last item you need to consider when writing this section is the differentiation of your work from related studies. This is very important, since it allows the reader to see the big picture of your study and how it furthers knowledge in this particular field.

The background and related work section should not read like a list of who did what. It should offer insights into and education about prior work, portraying recent developments in the field. It should help readers to understand previous work better than they did before. It is advisable to break this section into subsections, as this will enable the reader to grasp the various themes. For instance, if the paper introduces an adaptive game-based learning system for teaching mathematics, it is reasonable to report related work on (1) adaptive learning systems, (2) game-based learning, and (3) technology-assisted teaching of mathematics. The differentiation of the current work from prior work can then be achieved theme by theme, rather than by contrasting it with every piece of prior work under discussion.

The craft of writing this section lies in clarifying what has been done and how the study furthers knowledge. Thus, it is important to be able to formulate the differentiation positively, without being defensive in relation to previous work, and to maintain a narrative flow that nurtures readers' understanding. It is not necessary for the current work to assert itself as "better" than prior work; rather, it should be different than previous studies and should contribute adequately to an important research objective. This can take the form of asking a different question, using a different method or technique, building on different technological affordances, or focusing on different effects of these affordances (e.g., not necessarily to learning itself, but also to students' motivation and engagement). It is common for the last sentence of each paragraph to summarize the paragraph and provide insights to motivate the next paragraph. At the end of this section, it is important that the reader understands which gaps the study intends to bridge and the importance of doing so (i.e., the implications for research, theory, and practice).

Some venues might require a mini "literature review" section, but this is not required in all cases. You should bear in mind that this is not a literature review paper, and therefore related works that are not very close to the intended contribution may need to be ignored. This section should allow you to zoom in on the particular field. Zooming in too close (to an area with only two or three relevant studies) or not zooming in close enough (trying to describe all the relevant studies) will fail to provide the necessary information and narrative flow for the reader. Examples of related work sections that follow the aforementioned instructions can be seen in Lee-Cultura et al. (2020) and Giannakos et al. (2020).

7.3 Methods

The research methods employed must be described carefully, in great detail, and in line with accepted standards and conventions. As mentioned above, in the field of CCI and learning technology, forms of APA style are commonly used (APA, 2020). Therefore, drawing on our experience and on the guidelines and recommendations for various human-factors IT-related fields (e.g., Ko et al., 2015; Recker, 2012; Wobbrock, 2015; Ross & Morrison, 2013), we propose the following subsections outline that enables adequate description of methodological decisions. You may encounter small variations on the proposed outline, and differences are found between quantitative, qualitative, and mixed methods research studies. For example, qualitative research studies tend to use a wider range of structures than quantitative research studies. Nevertheless, there are certain essential methodological aspects and decisions that need to be covered, regardless of the nature of the research study. Therefore, the following subsections form part of a common structure found in most learning technology and CCI papers.

7.3.1 Participants

In this subsection, the researcher identifies particular characteristics (variables) of the participants in the study that are relevant to the study design. A typical participants subsection provides the number of participants, their genders, their mean age, their age variance, and the selection process and assignment (e.g., random selection or convenience sampling). An important element in this section is the description of the end-users; for instance, you should clarify the specific group of people you focus on (e.g., primary school students, teachers, or university students) and state your inclusion and exclusion criteria. You should also report whether and how participants were compensated. The rule of thumb is that you should give enough information for a similar group of users to be recruited in the future by an expert reader.

7.3.2 Setting/Procedure

This is normally the longest subsection within the method section, and it should describe the process participants went through during the treatment and data collection (e.g., for a lab study, from their arrival to their departure from the lab; for an in-the-wild study, the settings in the school or other environment). The researcher must identify where the data collection took place and provide details of the setting(s), which can be a single setting, various settings, or even some uncontrolled settings (as in experience sampling method studies). This section should detail what tasks the participants performed and in which order. It is important to provide enough detail for the expert reader to be able to replicate the study.

7.3 Methods

7.3.3 Data Collection

Researchers collect data in different ways. Whether the design is qualitative, quantitative, or mixed research, you need to describe what kind of data you have collected (e.g., log files, questionnaire data, sensor data, interviews, or field notes). Data collection is associated with specific measurements (which are associated with RQs). In some data collection methods (e.g., questionnaire data and some log files), the measurements are predefined; in others (e.g., sensor data), the measurements are post-computed; and in yet others (commonly in qualitative research studies), there are no measurements. In this subsection, you should report the data collection method and, if relevant, the measurements employed in the study.

7.3.4 Research Design

This subsection describes the experimental design and is a common feature of quantitative research studies and mixed methods research studies. A detailed description of experimental designs has been given in Chap. 4 of this volume (Common types of experimental designs). An effective practice for describing experiments with multiple treatments and/or groups is to set out the treatments and groups and their details. It is important to use the correct nomenclature and include all the necessary details. For example, we might state the following: It was a true experiment with an experimental group and a control group. The control group played a quiz (Kahoot!) at the end of each lecture that gave them feedback at the end of the quiz, whereas the experimental group played a quiz (Kahoot!) at the end of each lecture that gave them immediate feedback after each question. This research design investigates the effect of immediate feedback on students (e.g., performance and attitude).

7.3.5 Data Analysis

In quantitative studies, this subsection may be referred to statistical analysis, but you will normally see it referred to as data analysis. In this subsection, you must describe how the data collected were analyzed in order to answer the RQs (and/or test the hypotheses) of your paper. In other words, you should state what process you employed to make sense of the data you collected. If you collected quantitative data, you should describe the systematic process employed to analyze the numeric information collected, including the formal statistical analysis approach you took. For instance, you might state: "To investigate the effect of immediate feedback during the quiz on learning performance and students' attitudes, an independent samples t-test was applied between the control and experimental groups." You should also specify how the analyses were conducted (e.g., "The analyses were performed using SPSS 25.0 for Windows").

If qualitative data were collected, you will need to describe how they were analyzed. For instance, did you employ inductive or deductive coding? How were the themes identified? How did you arrive at your findings/results? How were objectivity and validity ensured? Did you adopt any "standard" processes (e.g., grounded theory)? If so, you need to describe in detail the procedures you followed for open coding, axial coding, selective coding, and theory formation, as well as providing the coding protocol (e.g., as an appendix or in an online repository). Did you use any reliability measurements (e.g., Cohen's kappa)? If so, what was the outcome? In general, the rule of thumb is that you should give enough detail for the analysis to be replicated by an expert reader if they have your data.

In a mixed methods research study, you should describe the aforementioned processes and add how you have triangulated your data (i.e., how you reached similar conclusions from different data sources and analyses). Triangulation can significantly strengthen the outcomes of your research, because it allows you to test your hypotheses and to explore ideas and experiences in depth.

7.4 Findings (or Results)

This section is used to report the findings (sometimes called the results) of the study. The findings come from the analysis of the data collected (Chap. 5 of this volume). No interpretation of the findings is made in this section. If the data were quantitative, the findings are reported numerically. If the data were qualitative, the findings are reported using narratives (usually quotations). If the data were quantitative and qualitative, both numeric and narrative representations are reported. The findings section speaks for itself: in it, you should report the results of your work in an organized way. The section refrains from discussing the importance of the results and from describing any potential implications; it focuses on reporting the results. Try to use charts, graphs, and tables as appropriate (for example, Fig. 7.2) and in line with the appropriate reporting conventions (https://www.socscistatistics.com/tutorials/test/default.aspx). Although you should refrain from discussing the results at this point, a well-written findings section has an easy-to-read narrative flow that allows the reader to grasp the answers to the RQs.

For quantitative research studies, the findings section can be divided into subsections that address different dependent variables or RQs. When including the results of statistical tests, you always need to use the appropriate conventions. For example, you can write: "An independent samples t-test was conducted to compare quiz scores for students who received immediate feedback and students' who received feedback at the end of the quiz" (as a reminder of which statistical test was used). Then, you will need to report the results clearly; for example, "The results show that there was a significant difference between the scores of students who received immediate feedback ($M = 54.99$, $SD = 8.13$) and those who received feedback at the

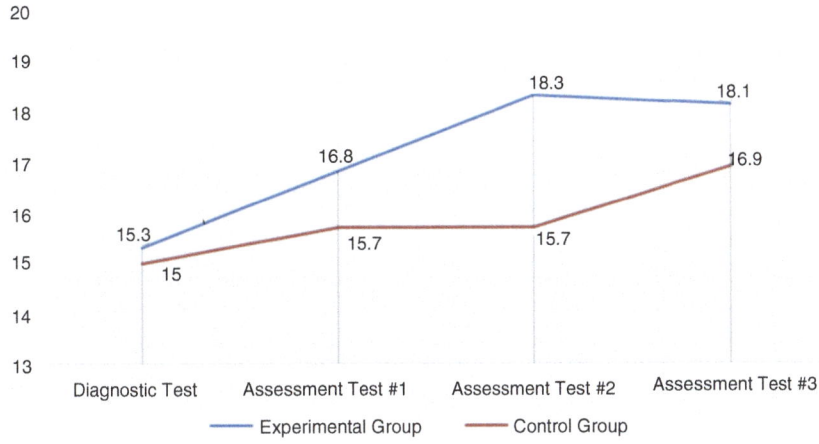

Fig. 7.2 Example of visualization of results comparing control and experimental groups

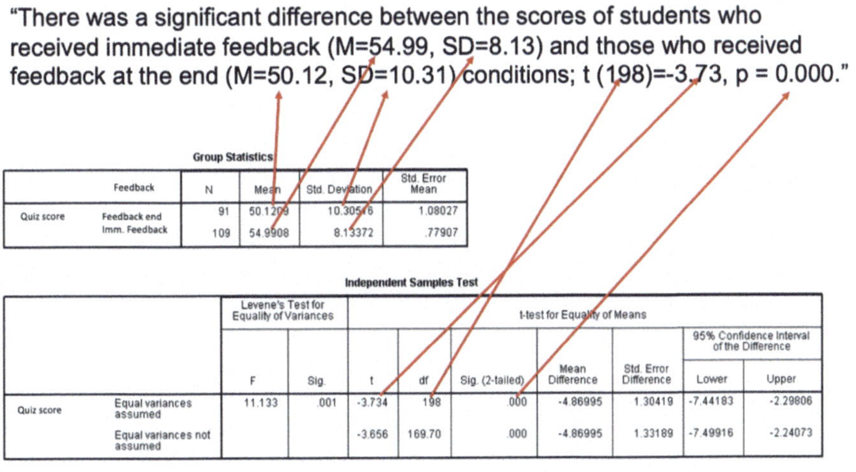

"There was a significant difference between the scores of students who received immediate feedback (M=54.99, SD=8.13) and those who received feedback at the end (M=50.12, SD=10.31) conditions; t (198)=-3.73, p = 0.000."

Group Statistics

	Feedback	N	Mean	Std. Deviation	Std. Error Mean
Quiz score	Feedback end	91	50.1209	10.30516	1.08027
	Imm. Feedback	109	54.9908	8.13372	.77907

Independent Samples Test

		Levene's Test for Equality of Variances		t-test for Equality of Means						
									95% Confidence Interval of the Difference	
		F	Sig.	t	df	Sig. (2-tailed)	Mean Difference	Std. Error Difference	Lower	Upper
Quiz score	Equal variances assumed	11.133	.001	-3.734	198	.000	-4.86995	1.30419	-7.44183	-2.29806
	Equal variances not assumed			-3.656	169.70	.000	-4.86995	1.33189	-7.49916	-2.24073

Fig. 7.3 Example reporting of independent samples t-test results from SPSS output

end of the quiz (M = 50.12, SD = 10.31) (t (198) = −3.73, p = 0.000)." Fig. 7.3 shows the output received from IBM SPSS software for this particular example and how you need to report it.

Supplementing statistical significance with descriptive statistics and effect sizes is very important, since it allows the reader to grasp the results better. The APA notes that it is "almost always necessary" to include effects sizes in the results section (APA, 2020). The effect size indicates the number of standard deviations by which the means of the experimental group differ from those of the control group. In the context of learning technology and CCI, an effect size (Cohen's d) of +0.8

indicates an important effect (i.e., a full standard deviation), while effect sizes of +0.2 and + 0.5 indicate small and medium effects, respectively (Cohen, 1988).

For qualitative field studies, there is a higher degree of freedom in reporting the results; however, the findings section is often divided into subsections according to the themes that emerged. The results sections may be quite long, incorporating notes and observations from the researchers as well as direct quotations from the participants (e.g., from the post-interview or from recordings made during the treatment). Organizing your results into subsections makes it easier for the reader to follow the flow of your paper.

Learning technology papers that adhere to the aforementioned conventions in the method and results sections include Ahn et al. (2018) and Hiniker et al. (2018) for qualitative research, Papamitsiou et al. (2019) and Papavlasopoulou et al. (2018) for quantitative research, and Watson et al. (2017) for mixed methods research. As you can see from these examples, although there is some degree of freedom in writing these sections, the specified general structure and content must be present.

7.5 Discussion

In the discussion section, the researcher interprets the results of the study. In the first paragraph, the researcher summarizes the main findings and relates them to the initial problem that the paper set out to address (i.e., the RQs). The summary of the findings and their connection to the RQs should come early in the discussion section. Then, the interpretation should begin. What do the results mean? What are the reasons behind the results? What do the results tell you in light of the relevant theory and/or related works? Each finding needs to be discussed in detail and interpreted against related published works. Does it confirm, disconfirm, or extend their results? This step is essential in demonstrating your research contribution (how your research adds to, complements, or clarifies the current body of knowledge). The goal of this section is to enable the reader to understand what your findings mean. Connections are usually made with the knowledge that was established in the introduction and related work sections, showing how your findings answer the RQs and bridge the knowledge gap you identified in the introduction. This is a very important part of the discussion, since it clarifies the contribution of your paper (i.e., what it adds to previously published works). Limited contribution is one of the most common reasons for a paper being rejected.

In other words, the discussion section reports what the results mean, what is interesting (novel) about them, and why they matter. The third part of the discussion, focused on why the results matter, is called the "implications" of the results. The implications part explains what the results mean, whether and how they influence current research and practice, and whether and how they will have any impact on theory. Although the discussion is not usually divided into subsections, it can be if it is long; in that case, the implications usually form a stand-alone subsection.

Another important part of the discussion that can be a stand-alone subsection is the limitations of the study. These are usually included at the end of the discussion section in the form of a paragraph or two summarizing the limitations caused by your methodological decisions. When selecting your method, there are always tradeoffs between the various decisions (e.g., research design and measurement instruments), and a mature and reflective researcher should state those limitations and view the results through that lens. In this section, it is important to avoid speculating about matters that do not emerge from the data collected. After limited contribution, speculation is the second most common sign of a low-quality discussion section. Good examples of learning technology and CCI papers that follow the abovementioned logic in the discussion section are Lee-Cultura et al. (2020) and Giannakos et al. (2020).

7.6 Conclusions and Further Research

This is a very short section (around two paragraphs) that addresses three points:

- It summarizes the contributions of the work and clarifies that you have delivered what has been promised in the RQs/introduction;
- It highlights any key points that you would like the reader to remember (i.e., the take-home message);
- It emphasizes the specific significance of the work and calls for future research that is likely to extend the reported study's findings (e.g., showing how this work opens avenues for new research).

Since the contributions have already been reported and discussed in previous sections, it is important to zoom out in this section and try to see the wood rather than the trees. You should avoid copying and pasting the text used in other sections to describe the contribution; however, limited repetition (such as rewriting some text in a simplified manner) may be appropriate. Try to frame the contributions of the work in such a way that their value can be understood by a generalist, not just by researchers of this particular narrow topic.

The last paragraph of this section describes the avenues for future research that have been opened by your results and calls for studies that will extend, complement, or exploit your findings. In some cases, researchers use this part to describe their own future research. It is often better to suggest a few well-considered and important future steps than a "mainstream" list of smaller items (e.g., collecting additional data or implementing a similar study).

References

Ahn, J., Clegg, T., Yip, J., Bonsignore, E., Pauw, D., Cabrera, L., ... & Marr, R. (2018). Science everywhere: Designing public, tangible displays to connect youth learning across settings. In *Proceedings of the 2018 CHI conference on human factors in computing* systems (pp. 1–12).

APA. (2020). *Publication manual of the American Psychological Association: The official guide to APA style* (7th ed.). American Psychological Association.

Cohen, J. (1988). *Statistical power analysis for the behavioral sciences* (2nd ed.). Erlbaum.

Giannakos, M. N., Sharma, K., Papavlasopoulou, S., Pappas, I. O., & Kostakos, V. (2020). Fitbit for learning: Towards capturing the learning experience using wearable sensing. *International Journal of Human-Computer Studies, 136*, 102384.

Hiniker, A., Heung, S. S., Hong, S., & Kientz, J. A. (2018). Coco's videos: An empirical investigation of video-player design features and children's media use. In *Proceedings of the 2018 CHI conference on human factors in computing systems* (pp. 1–13).

Ko, A. J., LaToza, T. D., & Burnett, M. M. (2015). A practical guide to controlled experiments of software engineering tools with human participants. *Empirical Software Engineering, 20*(1), 110–141.

Lee-Cultura, S., Sharma, K., Papavlasopoulou, S., Retalis, S., & Giannakos, M. (2020). Using sensing technologies to explain children's self-representation in motion-based educational games. In *Proceedings of the interaction design and children conference* (pp. 541–555).

Papamitsiou, Z., Economides, A. A., & Giannakos, M. N. (2019). Fostering learners' performance with on-demand metacognitive feedback. In *European conference on technology enhanced learning* (pp. 423–435). Springer.

Papavlasopoulou, S., Sharma, K., & Giannakos, M. N. (2018). How do you feel about learning to code? Investigating the effect of children's attitudes towards coding using eye-tracking. *International Journal of Child-Computer Interaction, 17*, 50–60.

Recker, J. (2012). *Scientific research in information systems: A beginner's guide*. Springer Science & Business Media.

Ross, S. M., & Morrison, G. R. (2013). Experimental research methods. In *Handbook of research on educational communications and technology* (pp. 1007–1029). Routledge.

Watson, S. L., Watson, W. R., Yu, J. H., Alamri, H., & Mueller, C. (2017). Learner profiles of attitudinal learning in a MOOC: An explanatory sequential mixed methods study. *Computers & Education, 114*, 274–285.

Wobbrock, J. O. (2015). *Catchy titles are good: But avoid being cute.* https://gangw.cs.illinois.edu/Wobbrock-2015.pdf.

Open Access This chapter is licensed under the terms of the Creative Commons Attribution 4.0 International License (http://creativecommons.org/licenses/by/4.0/), which permits use, sharing, adaptation, distribution and reproduction in any medium or format, as long as you give appropriate credit to the original author(s) and the source, provide a link to the Creative Commons license and indicate if changes were made.

The images or other third party material in this chapter are included in the chapter's Creative Commons license, unless indicated otherwise in a credit line to the material. If material is not included in the chapter's Creative Commons license and your intended use is not permitted by statutory regulation or exceeds the permitted use, you will need to obtain permission directly from the copyright holder.

Chapter 8
Common Criteria, Pitfalls, and Practices in CCI and Learning Technology Research

Abstract Thus far, the book provides materials to carry out the whole process of observation, rationalization, and validation, as well as the necessary supporting processes (e.g., artifact design, data analysis, and reporting). At the end of the process, everything is documented in a comprehensive report or a paper, and the respective prototypes, datasets, and practical information are kept on file. An important question, however, remains: In the context of CCI and learning technology research, what are the main reasons for reviewers rejecting a paper or asking for revisions? Considerable effort goes into preparing a paper contribution for a respectable venue (journal or a conference). Researchers do not want to see their effort go to waste, especially if it involves a potentially valuable contribution that could bring credit to authors and fresh insights to readers. Drawing on our own experience and on various guides on how to review papers in CCI, learning technology, and neighboring fields, in this chapter we provide a list of criteria and pitfalls that are common to CCI and learning technology venues.

Keywords Criteria · Pitfalls · Review · Learning technology · Child-computer interaction

8.1 Common Criteria

The above materials give you enough information to carry out the whole process of observation, rationalization, and validation, as well as the necessary supporting processes (e.g., artefact design, data analysis, and reporting). At the end of the process, everything is documented in a comprehensive report or a paper, and the respective prototypes, datasets, and practical information are kept on file. An important question, however, remains: In the context of CCI and learning technology research, what are the main reasons for reviewers rejecting a paper or asking for revisions? Drawing on our own experience and on various guides on how to review papers in CCI, learning technology, and neighboring fields (e.g., HCI,[1] CSCW,[2] and RLT[3]), we believe that the following criteria and pitfalls are common to CCI and learning technology venues (although their relative importance and level of explicitness may vary).

The following list gives the most common criteria applied when reviewing papers in CCI and learning technology venues.

- **Relevance.** Substantive research and/or design knowledge contributions should be concerned with "the phenomena surrounding the interaction between children and computational and communication technologies" (for CCI) and "advances in learning technologies and their applications" (for learning technology). Simply using children as end-users or a technology that might be able to support learning to study a general or educational phenomenon is generally not enough.
- **Importance/significance.** Research should address a significant problem of important and lasting value. This criterion can be met by, for example, motivating RQs or hypotheses in terms of learning or HCI theory, by interpreting results in such terms, or by responding to a challenge that has been discussed and debated in the literature.
- **Grounding in the literature.** Grounding in prior research literature is very important. A reference list that seems to omit the most important works or is extremely short could be grounds for desk rejection (i.e., because of the paper's obvious lack of relevance/thoroughness/importance, the editor decides not to send it for peer review).
- **Scientific rigor.** A paper should use methodology that is appropriate for the RQs. A general report on the experience of a practitioner or an instructor in implementing an innovation, or an obscure form of data collection, is generally not enough.
- **Write-up and structure.** A paper must be clearly written in appropriate language and be properly structured (e.g., Introduction, Related work, Methods, Findings, Discussion, Conclusion).
- **Research ethics.** There should be some discussion of the ethics of working with children as research participants/teachers/partners (whenever this is relevant). For example, has approval from an ethics board (or institutional review board, IRB) been obtained for the research? If not, it is common to reject the paper immediately and not allow resubmission until a statement of approval has been obtained.

These criteria are commonly used by editors, program chairs, and reviewers to evaluate a paper in the area of CCI and learning technology. It is necessary to weigh up the criteria realistically; for example, a paper that is not well-written may nevertheless contain important results. However, it is important for papers to satisfy most of the criteria, with the potential to satisfy all of them after revision.

---

[1] CHI guide: https://chi2021.acm.org/for-authors/presenting/papers/guide-to-a-successful-submission
[2] CSCW guide: http://cscw.acm.org/2016/volunteer/DaveRandallReviewingforCSCW.pdf
[3] *Research in Learning Technology (RLT)* journal: https://journal.alt.ac.uk/index.php/rlt/reviewers

8.2 Potential Pitfalls

Along with the aforementioned criteria, it is important to be aware of pitfalls when designing, conducting, and reporting CCI and learning technology studies. The following list gives the most common pitfalls in such research.

- **Insufficient theoretical base, literature grounding, or rationale.** The basis for a study is the formulation of certain RQs or hypotheses from a relevant theoretical base, previously published studies, and/or a rationale and argumentation from the researcher's observations. Most studies use a combination of theory, related work, and rationale to ground their hypotheses and provide rock-solid motivation. **Example:** Observations conducted throughout the semester on students who used adaptive assessment questions (questions that are assigned to students by taking into consideration what they have mastered and the difficulty of the questions) and relevant theoretical concepts (e.g., zone of proximal development and flow state) motivate our work on the benefits of adaptive content. Therefore, we hypothesize that students who receive adaptive content will have significantly better LPS than students who receive content procedurally.
- **Low internal validity of conditions and/or subjects.** Conditions and/or subjects are not uniformly implemented, such that certain groups have an advantage on a particular condition. **Example:** The experimental group receives a task/condition that needs less time to be processed (low internal validity of condition), or the experimental group consists of older students who have more developed cognitive skills (e.g., faster reading speeds). Other reasons for low internal validity include a lack of randomization (e.g., allowing students to select the group they join, such that high performers might select the experimental group) and developing unequal treatments.
- **Failure of the developed artefact to support the intended testing.** This is a common pitfall for CCI and learning technology studies. Artifacts have a certain set of qualities or components (e.g., functionalities and affordances) that allow us to experiment by isolating and testing certain components. Nevertheless, when artifacts fail to isolate the components we intended, we introduce bias or confounds (mixing the effect of the exposure of primary interest with extraneous risk factors). As a result, we cannot test effectively the components we want to test. **Example:** The study introduces a visual dashboard that presents different information compared to the nonvisual (control) dashboard. Therefore, the researcher cannot determine whether the observed effects are associated with the different information presented or the visualization of the dashboard.
- **Measurement bias.** Variables and other outcomes are not measured in a proper scientific way (as when, in a qualitative study, no standardized scales are used, or when, in a quantitative study, observations and analysis are carried out by the single author without any reliability checks). **Example:** In a quantitative study, the measures employed do not correspond to the variable in the research question, or they can be interpreted from the participants' responses in different ways. This situation would arise in a qualitative study of teachers' use of technology

where the researcher who conducted the observations of the teachers was also working as a teacher in the same school.
- **Low external validity (low/no generalization).** The topic is not important, or the results are weak and not generalizable to other contexts. Low external validity makes it more difficult to identify potential implications than in an externally valid study, and this limits the contribution to the literature. Nevertheless, it is important to emphasize that a study (e.g., a laboratory-based study) may have low external validity but high internal validity, and some types of journals welcome such studies.
- **Trivial outcomes.** The outcomes of the study constitute a "self-fulfilling prophecy." **Example:** A group of students at a formal operational stage (aged 12 and over) perform mathematical operations faster than a group of students who are at a concrete operational stage (aged 7–11).
- **Problems with data analysis.** The analyses necessary to address the RQs are not applied properly or are not well described. **Example:** A quantitative study uses statistical tests that depend on certain parametric assumptions, but the authors did not check whether those assumptions were met; or although the RQs require statistical analysis of causal effects, the authors have conducted correlational analyses instead.
- **Poor writing or inadequate description of methodology.** This problem arises when the writing style is unclear, the language quality (syntax) is poor, the paper is badly structured, and/or important methodological details have been omitted. **Examples:** The method section contains no subheadings and mixes the variables, descriptions of participants, and analysis; the results are presented in a very opinionated manner (mixed with discussion); the discussion section is missing (i.e., there is no interpretation of the results); or obvious limitations of the selected methodology are not discussed.

8.3 Useful Practices

There are several detailed guides to help learning technology and CCI researchers to understand how to carry out their research and provide them with appropriate practices and approaches (e.g., Hudson & Mankoff, 2014; McKenney & Reeves, 2018). In the introduction to this book, we also describe the main steps of the research process. The purpose of this section is slightly different, namely to offer some practical advice to new CCI and learning technology researchers.

When planning your research, it is important to be able to provide a visual summary of your research design and the underlying idea. As the researcher, you should be able to provide a brief but clear motivation for the proposed research and your methodological decisions. Your motivation can be supported by related work and learning/HCI theories. Typical questions to ask yourself at this step include: What is the main motivation and goal of this research? Is the idea materialized with a technological or other innovation? What does the literature say? For instance, your

8.3 Useful Practices

motivation might be to provide timely feedback to your students, and therefore you want to test a new clicker technology that provides immediate feedback, unlike previous technologies that only provide summary feedback at the end of the class hour.

Next, you need to formulate your RQs clearly, so that they are properly scoped and capable of being answered. For instance, what is the role of immediate feedback in students' learning performance and attitude during lectures? You then need to think of your target population (e.g., university students), the instruments and data collection methods you want to use (e.g., log data or pre-post survey), the analysis methods you expect to use (e.g., independent t-test on students' response times), and the outcomes you expect to find (e.g., students will respond more slowly but their accuracy and attitude will improve). At the end of this exercise, you will have a summary like Table 8.1 that allows you to reflect on, explain, and discuss your research proposal.

Although this is not a comprehensive technique for representing a detailed research proposition, it is a practical way to summarize and communicate your proposal. Similar diagrams have been recommended in support of different goals (e.g., writing proposals for funding MSc/PhD thesis studies) and different stages of research (e.g., brainstorming or data analysis).[4]

---

[4] https://medium.com/@markguzdial/defining-a-proposal-in-one-table-how-to-write-a-blumenfeld-chart-927a4dcf5dcb#.wzil65yuc

Table 8.1 Overview of data analysis procedures used in learning technology and CCI research

Motivation	Artefact	Research question	Participants	Instruments	Analysis	Expected results
Providing timely feedback to students, allowing them to reflect upon their performance during the lecture and increase their attention, performance, and positive attitude, but reducing their response times	Adding a small pop-up dashboard at the end of each question giving the student the basic information	Does the introduction of immediate feedback improve students' attention, performance, attitude, and response rate when using clickers in the classroom?	A sample of participants from the introductory programming course will be asked to participate. They will be assigned at random to group A or group B. In group A (experimental group), the clicker application will present a pop-up dashboard after each question, whereas in group B (control group), the application will not present the dashboard.	Correctness, based on clicker log files. Response time, based on clicker log files. Post-class attitudinal and attentional survey	Independent t-test on students' response times, response correctness, and attitudinal and attentional survey responses	Immediate feedback will increase students' correctness, attitude, and attention during the class, but it will also increase their response time.

References

Hudson, S. E., & Mankoff, J. (2014). Concepts, values, and methods for technical human–computer interaction research. In *Ways of knowing in HCI* (pp. 69–93). Springer.

McKenney, S., & Reeves, T. C. (2018). *Conducting educational design research*. Routledge.

Open Access This chapter is licensed under the terms of the Creative Commons Attribution 4.0 International License (http://creativecommons.org/licenses/by/4.0/), which permits use, sharing, adaptation, distribution and reproduction in any medium or format, as long as you give appropriate credit to the original author(s) and the source, provide a link to the Creative Commons license and indicate if changes were made.

The images or other third party material in this chapter are included in the chapter's Creative Commons license, unless indicated otherwise in a credit line to the material. If material is not included in the chapter's Creative Commons license and your intended use is not permitted by statutory regulation or exceeds the permitted use, you will need to obtain permission directly from the copyright holder.

Chapter 9
Developments in Data Science and Artificial Intelligence in Learning Technology and CCI Research

Abstract This book is focusing on experimental studies in learning technology and CCI research. During the last years, the areas of data science and AI have influenced different aspects of human-factors IT-related research in general and learning technology and CCI research in particular. Therefore, although this book does not provide a deep discussion on how data science and AI have influenced contemporary learning technology and CCI research; in this chapter, we provide a brief presentation of the developments in data science and AI, and the role of those developments in learning technology and CCI research.

Keywords Data science · Artificial intelligence · Learning technology · Multimodal data

9.1 Data Science

Most CCI and learning technology studies are conducted on small groups of participants, often from a homogeneous context (e.g., the same school or a similar background). With the emergence of online education and learning-at-scale technologies (e.g., MOOCs, LMSs, ITSs, open courseware, and community tutorial systems such as Stack Overflow), millions of participants in different parts of the world and from different backgrounds can engage with CCI and learning technology systems. New forms of data require new methodologies. As we have described in this book, a classical approach in a CCI and learning technology study would involve some dozens of end-users participating in each condition and would apply hypothesis-testing analysis (e.g., t-tests or ANOVAs). Since the datasets (and the respective data points) would be small, only large effects would be detectable, and so significance would imply relevance. On the other hand, if the number of students is large, we could easily end up rejecting the null hypothesis and detecting an effect that is irrelevant in practice (Kidzinski et al., 2016).

As mentioned above, in CCI and learning technology research, typical data analysis techniques (e.g., analysis of variance, correlations, and regressions) are usually employed to explore the RQs and test the hypotheses, where the formulation of the RQs and the hypothesis formation are guided by previous work and/or theories. However, when dealing with massive amounts of data (e.g., from MOOCs or LMSs) or rich multimodal data (e.g., video, eye-tracking, or other sensor data), different statistical analysis techniques need to be employed (including predictions and classifications). Given that learning/educational scientists and designers are often unfamiliar with contemporary modeling techniques, this has prompted an increasing number of computer scientists, statisticians, and data scientists to engage with CCI and learning technology research. In many cases, because of the nature of the problem and the data (e.g., online learning), contextual knowledge (e.g., how someone is using YouTube or Stack Overflow in their learning) is either not relevant or cannot be captured (e.g., in a MOOC). In such cases, we see research initiatives in CCI and learning technology that seek to address problems in the absence of contextual knowledge.

This type of decontextualized and large-scale experimentation in CCI and learning technology research lies outside the scope of this book. However, we would like to emphasize that exploratory data analysis techniques (Tukey, 1977) can be useful, particularly for finding an adequate data transformation and for outlier detections. Explorations of this type can bring new insights and hypotheses and eventually close the cycle (see Fig. 9.1). For those interested in how to employ advanced data science and machine learning (ML) techniques in the context of learning, we provide elsewhere a mini-tutorial on methodologies for forming and testing hypotheses in large educational datasets (Kidzinski et al., 2016). We also present practical guidance for building data-driven predictive models with state-of-the-art ML methods, using the R and CARET packages because of their simplicity and the ease of access to the most recent ML methods.

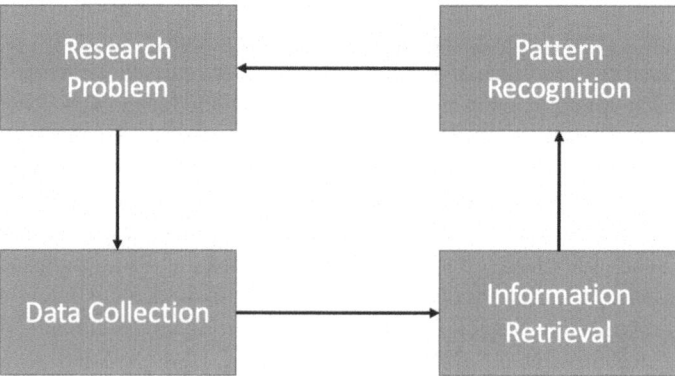

Fig. 9.1 Data-driven CCI and learning technology in at-scale contexts. (Adapted from Kidzinski et al., 2016)

9.2 Artificial Intelligence

Artificial intelligence (AI) in CCI and learning technology research is traditionally represented by AI in education (AIED), intelligent user interfaces (IUI), and the ITS communities, and involves a wide spectrum of technologies and approaches. In recent years, we have seen AI technologies and approaches employed in almost every CCI and learning technology community. Since the 1980s, researchers have been interested in the association between learning and AI, although initially this mainly meant a focus on knowledge representation, reasoning, and learning (Self, 2015, p. 5). Russell and Norvig (2021) have described AI as a technology that includes problem solving, representation, reasoning on the basis of certain/uncertain knowledge, ML, and communicating, perceiving, and acting techniques for designing and developing intelligent agents. More recently, we have seen various developments in sensing technologies, analytics, and visualization, as well as cognitive technologies and architectures that have boosted the use of AI to support teaching and learning. The *International Journal of Artificial Intelligence in Education* (IJAIED[1]) describes the focus of the AIED field as the development and design of AI-powered computer-based learning systems, including agent-based learning environments, Bayesian and other statistical methods, cognitive tools for learning, intelligent agents on the Internet, natural language interfaces for instructional systems, and real-world applications of AIED systems.

The topic of AI and advanced data science techniques in education is not central to this book; nevertheless given recent advances in data science, this book would not be complete if we did not introduce the reader to these advancements. Drawing from a recent literature review on AIED (Chen et al., 2020), we see that contemporary AI learning systems incorporate various techniques and technologies, such as recommendations, knowledge understanding and ML, data mining, and knowledge models (Avella et al., 2016). There are three main components of an AI-powered learning system: the educational data collections from learners' and teachers' activities, the techniques or modeling employed (e.g., knowledge inference or ML), and the system's intelligence as expressed through different intelligent technologies (Kim et al., 2018). Figure 9.2 shows how these three components work together to enable AI functionalities in the learning system.

As Fig. 9.2 makes clear, the quality of data collection is of paramount importance if an AI learning system is to operate efficiently. In the context of CCI, we see children's toys evolving through advances in embedded electronics, digital capabilities, and wireless connectivity that combine different capabilities such as networking, processing, and intelligent reasoning. As we see from a recent *IJCCI* special issue in AI and CCI,[2] the increasing use of such interactive objects in CCI and the rise of

---

[1] *International Journal of Artificial Intelligence in Education*: https://www.springer.com/journal/40593

[2] https://www.sciencedirect.com/journal/international-journal-of-child-computer-interaction/special-issue/103G37QK1KT

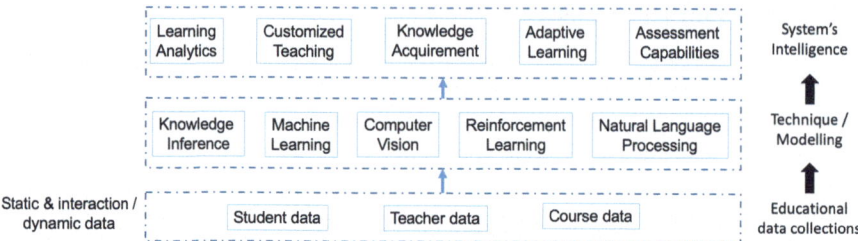

Fig. 9.2 Representation of AI-powered educational systems, which consists of the data collections layer (e.g., educational and interaction data), the modeling techniques which developing different intelligence based on the data collections, and the system's intelligence part that provides the technologies needs to provide the intelligence as a service to the user

AI techniques through data-driven methods reinforce intelligent features and adaptivity, but they also bring many significant privacy issues and ethical concerns.

In summary, AI technologies can amplify different areas of human abilities, including physical, memory, perception, cognition and learning (Shneiderman, 2020). Examples of technologies that leverage AI to amplify human abilities are, information representation/ awareness/ reflection technologies (e.g., dashboards), in-situ human-computer interaction technologies (e.g., augmented reality and ubiquitous displays), and technologies with implicit and adaptive control (e.g., gaze tracking). On the contrary of autonomous AI systems that focus on replacing human decision making, those AI technologies employ the notion of "intelligence augmentation" (IA) that attempts to support human abilities (e.g., decision making, cognition) rather than replacing them. Contemporary learning systems employ different information representation and IA techniques via powerful interfaces and communication modalities (e.g., dashboards, adaptive navigation). Those interfaces and communication modalities combine various log data and provide explicit, easy-to-understand, and concise ways of presenting valuable information to support human abilities.

9.3 Sensor Data and Multimodal Learning Analytics

The use of sensors to support research on human-factors IT-related fields (especially in the context of learning) is not new. To some extent, the use of sensors (e.g., via cameras) has been central to LS research for several decades, as the popularity of qualitative video analysis indicates. However, in recent years, a proliferation of wearable and remote devices has made sensing widely available and affordable in the context of education, and a growing number of related studies have been published (Sharma & Giannakos, 2020). In addition, new methods, models, and algorithms have been developed (Blikstein & Worsley, 2016) that enable the continuous, unobtrusive, automated, and useful application of sensors during learning. Thanks to these devices and techniques, it is possible to monitor indices that are argued to

9.3 Sensor Data and Multimodal Learning Analytics

be significant for learning but have often been ignored because of the difficulties of measuring and interpreting them dynamically (Giannakos et al., 2020). Despite the challenges of using sensor data, previous studies have advocated the use of sensor technologies to capture complex interactions exchanged between learners/children and the interactive systems they engage with (Giannakos et al., 2022). Work on quantified-self movement has shown potential in using sensor data to support human decision making (e.g., in relation to diet, fitness, and lifestyle), self-monitoring, self-awareness, and self-reflection (Qi et al., 2018), as well as potential in learning technology (Giannakos et al., 2020) and CCI research (Lee-Cultura et al., 2020).

Research on collecting, pre-processing (e.g., data "cleaning"), synchronizing, and analyzing sensor data streams can be found in neighboring fields such as HCI and ubiquitous computing, with applications dating from the 1980s onward (Weiser et al., 1999). Sensor data has also been at the center of several learning technology and HCI communities, such as ITS (D'Mello et al., 2010), educational data mining (EDM) (Romero et al., 2010), and user modeling, adaptation, and personalization (UMAP) (Desmarais & Baker, 2012). The typical steps when using sensors include data collection, pre-processing, engineering, mining/analysis, validation, contextualization, and making sense of the results. These steps are somewhat different depending on whether there is a data-driven or a theory/hypothesis-driven approach, on the research design employed (e.g., qualitative or quantitative), and on the epistemic stance of the researchers (e.g., positivist or post-positivist) (Giannakos et al., 2022). In the last decade, there has been much discussion around the use of sensors in learning technology and CCI (Giannakos et al., 2022; Markopoulos et al., 2021), with different communities using different nomenclature to describe various facets of sensor data (e.g., sensor data in education, sensing, physiological analytics, ubiquitous data in education, and multimodal learning analytics).

In a recent chapter focusing on the use of sensor data in education (Giannakos et al., 2022), the authors described the advantages and qualities of sensor data in terms of three pillars. First and foremost, whereas computer logs enable us to capture learners' actions in binary fashion, sensors go further in terms of richness, allowing us to capture information about learners regardless of whether they have completed an action (e.g., while watching a video but not interacting with it, or interacting with a nondigital object). Second, sensors provide temporality by being sensitive to temporal changes and giving us direct access to indices that are relevant to cognitive and affective processes. Third, instead of reductive representation of the user and learner experience, sensor data provide granularity, allowing us to capture very low-level insights and focus our analysis on different aspects. Those qualities of sensor data, combined with advances in data science and AI, can provide powerful learning capabilities. For instance, they can provide access to indices relevant to cognitive and affective processes (see Fig. 9.3, left), or they can incorporate sensor data into a learning system's functionality (e.g., embodiment) or intelligence (e.g., affective support) via appropriate technological architectures (see Fig. 9.3, right).

To summarize this chapter, sensor data have several qualities that support interaction with the technology. Many of those qualities are beneficial for learning systems and can help us to improve the effectiveness of those systems. At the same

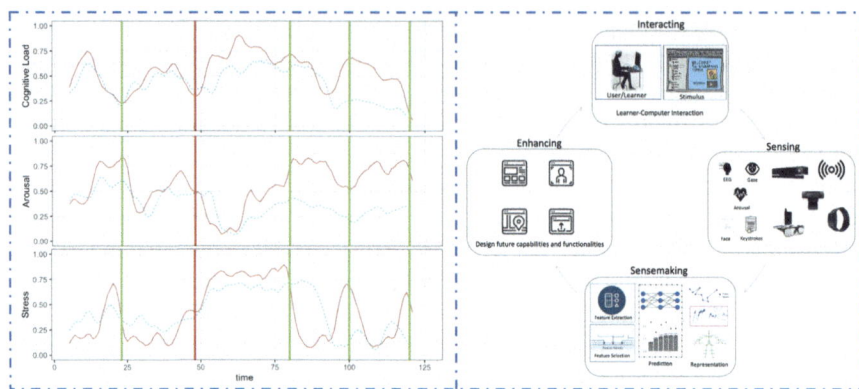

Fig. 9.3 Meaningful sensor data from a child interacting with a learning technology. (From Giannakos et al., 2021; with permission by IEEE). Left: The vertical lines show the child's response correctness (green for correct, red for incorrect), the solid red curves show the child's indices, and the dashed-green curves show the average for the whole class. Right: The logic of a system that leverages sensor data

time, sensor data introduce challenges that need to be tackled to allow contemporary learning technology research and practice to realize the potential benefits. Contemporary research on sensor data and advanced computational analyses has introduced the term "multimodal learning analytics" (MMLA) and led to the formation of the a special interest group in the context of the Society for Learning Analytics Research (SoLAR).[3]

References

Avella, J. T., Kebritchi, M., Nunn, S. G., & Kanai, T. (2016). Learning analytics methods, benefits, and challenges in higher education: A systematic literature review. *Online Learning, 20*(2), 13–29.

Blikstein, P., & Worsley, M. (2016). Multimodal learning analytics and education data mining: Using computational technologies to measure complex learning tasks. *Journal of Learning Analytics, 3*(2), 220–238.

Chen, L., Chen, P., & Lin, Z. (2020). Artificial intelligence in education: A review. *IEEE Access, 8*, 75264–75278.

D'Mello, S., Lehman, B., Sullins, J., Daigle, R., Combs, R., Vogt, K., Perkins, L., & Graesser, A. (2010). A time for emoting: When affect-sensitivity is and isn't effective at promoting deep learning. In *International conference on intelligent tutoring systems* (pp. 245–254).

Desmarais, M. C., & Baker, R. S. (2012). A review of recent advances in learner and skill modeling in intelligent learning environments. *User Modeling and User-AdaptedInteraction, 22*(1), 9–38.

Giannakos, M. N., Sharma, K., Papavlasopoulou, S., Pappas, I. O., & Kostakos, V. (2020). Fitbit for learning: Towards capturing the learning experience using wearable sensing. *International Journal of Human-Computer Studies, 136*, 102384.

---

[3] SoLAR CrossMMLA SIG: https://www.solaresearch.org/community/sigs/crossmmla-sig/

References

Giannakos, M. N., Lee-Cultura, S., & Sharma, K. (2021). Sensing-based analytics in education: The rise of multimodal data enabled learning systems. *IT Professional*. doi: 10.1109/MITP.2021.3089659.

Giannakos, M., Cukurova, M., & Papavlasopoulou, S. (2022). Sensor-based analytics in education: Lessons learned from research in multimodal learning analytics. In M. Giannakos, D. Spikol, D. DiMitri, K. Sharma, X. Ochoa & R. Hammad (Eds.). The Multimodal Learning Analytics Handbook. Springer.

Kidziński, Ł., Giannakos, M., Sampson, D. G., & Dillenbourg, P. (2016). A tutorial on machine learning in educational science. In *State-of-the-art and future directions of smart learning* (pp. 453–459). Springer.

Kim, Y., Soyata, T., & Behnagh, R. F. (2018). Towards emotionally aware AI smart classroom: Current issues and directions for engineering and education. *IEEE Access, 6*, 5308–5331.

Lee-Cultura, S., Sharma, K., Papavlasopoulou, S., Retalis, S., & Giannakos, M. (2020). Using sensing technologies to explain children's self-representation in motion-based educational games. In Proceedings of the interaction design and children conference (pp. 541–555).

Markopoulos, P., Read, J., & Giannakos, M. (2021). Design of digital technologies for children. In G. Salvendy & W. Karwowski (Eds.), *Handbook of human factors and ergonomics* (5th ed.). Wiley.

Qi, J., Yang, P., Waraich, A., Deng, Z., Zhao, Y., & Yang, Y. (2018). Examining sensor-based physical activity recognition and monitoring for healthcare using internet of things: A systematic review. *Journal of Biomedical Informatics, 87*, 138–153.

Romero, C., Ventura, S., Pechenizkiy, M., & Baker, R. S. (2010). *Handbook of educational data mining*. CRC Press.

Russell, S., & Norvig, P. (2021). *Artificial intelligence: A modern approach, global* (Vol. 19, 4th ed., p. 23). Pearson.

Self, J. (2015). The birth of IJAIED. *International Journal of Artificial Intelligence in Education, 26*(1), 4–12.

Sharma, K., & Giannakos, M. (2020). Multimodal data capabilities for learning: What can multimodal data tell us about learning? *British Journal of Educational Technology, 51*(5), 1450–1484.

Shneiderman, B. (2020). Human-centered artificial intelligence: Reliable, safe & trustworthy. *International Journal of Human–Computer Interaction, 36*(6), 495–504.

Tukey, J. W. (1977). *Exploratory data analysis* (Vol. 2, pp. 131–160).

Weiser, M., Gold, R., & Brown, J. S. (1999). The origins of ubiquitous computing research at parc in the late 1980s. *IBM Systems Journal, 38*(4), 693–696.

Open Access This chapter is licensed under the terms of the Creative Commons Attribution 4.0 International License (http://creativecommons.org/licenses/by/4.0/), which permits use, sharing, adaptation, distribution and reproduction in any medium or format, as long as you give appropriate credit to the original author(s) and the source, provide a link to the Creative Commons license and indicate if changes were made.

The images or other third party material in this chapter are included in the chapter's Creative Commons license, unless indicated otherwise in a credit line to the material. If material is not included in the chapter's Creative Commons license and your intended use is not permitted by statutory regulation or exceeds the permitted use, you will need to obtain permission directly from the copyright holder.

Chapter 10
Issues to Consider as a CCI and Learning Technology Researcher

Abstract In this chapter, we present three topics that are of great importance to CCI and learning technology researchers. The first topic is concerned with the role of "context" in experimental studies, and CCI and learning technology in general. The second topic is concerned with the ethical considerations in experimentation in human-factors IT-related research. The third topic focuses on researchers conducting experimental studies with children, and the need to employ different methods, approaches, and techniques. Although those are the three topics I decided to include in this book, I also believe that additional topics can complement this list.

Keywords Learning technology · Child-computer interaction · Context · Ethics · Children

10.1 Context in Experimental Studies

CCI and learning technology research is commonly constructed in the interplay of actors (learners, children, teachers, and parents), activities, and technology. It is informed by theory, conducted following experimental research methods, and reflects on epistemological stances. In most cases, the research is situated in particular contexts, which may be cultural, technological, infrastructural, or organizational. With the ultimate objective of making discoveries and contributing new and valid knowledge, the research can have significant implications for how people live and learn in technology-rich environments. Therefore, the knowledge obtained needs to be relevant and useful (i.e., contextualized) (Davison & Martinsons, 2016), as well as carrying a certain degree of validity (i.e., generalizability) (Cheng et al., 2016).

Validity in research is often referred to in terms of generalizability and universalizability. A definition that is easy to understand and adequate for the learning technology and CCI fields calls validity the "act of arguing, by induction, that there is a reasonable expectation that a knowledge claim already believed to be true in one or more settings is also true in other clearly defined settings" (Seddon & Scheepers, 2012). In learning technology and CCI, researchers may generalize knowledge in various ways, such as from one learning design to another, from one educational level to another, from one culture to another, from one context to the development of a new theory, and from one context to the extension of an existing theory. The same is true of other human-factors IT-related fields (Lee & Baskerville, 2012). However, an important question that is often posed in those fields is whether validity can reasonably be expected to extend to other contexts, given the well-defined contexts in which most research is conducted (Davison & Martinsons, 2016; Cheng et al., 2016).

The importance of contextualization and generalizability (sometimes referred to as particularism and universalism) has been extensively debated in several research fields (e.g., Deaton, 2010; Lee & Baskerville, 2012; Davison & Martinsons, 2016; Cheng et al., 2016). There has been a similar discussion in the field of learning technologies and HCI, with some studies focusing on achieving generalizability of their results (Sao Pedro et al., 2013) and others on producing contextually rich findings (Ferguson et al., 2014). There is general recognition that knowledge comes in various forms, ranging from highly general knowledge (e.g., universal laws) to highly contextualized insights (Höök et al., 2015; Höök & Löwgren, 2012). In addition, in the field of learning technologies, there are subcommunities (e.g., LAK and EDM) that adopt different stances and observe nuances in those two notions (Siemens & Baker, 2012). Regardless of one's stance toward those two very important notions, it is generally agreed that context matters in learning technologies and CCI research, and the importance of generalizability should not be downplayed. Researchers need to understand the research context fully, as this, in combination with replication and triangulation, can contribute to the (cautious) construction of intermediate- and higher-level knowledge (Polit & Beck, 2010) of how humans learn, play, communicate, and live in technology-rich environments.

Because of the data-intensive nature of contemporary research and its focus on interventions (e.g., collecting LMS analytics, as opposed to older relatively static approaches such as end-of-treatment surveys or interviews), the notions of contextualization and generalizability are of particular importance. Contemporary data collection has the capacity to bridge those two notions by reinforcing their complementarities, rather than contributing to a debate that treats them as two antagonistic notions. In particular, the capabilities of automated data collections (Sharma & Giannakos, 2020) afford a high degree of context-awareness (e.g., GPS, motion trackers, and accelerometers) and generalizability (e.g., measures with high internal and external validity, such as eye-tracking). Seminal work (Sharma et al., 2020) has provided evidence of the ability to support both context-awareness and generalizability. Therefore, learner and user analytics have the capacity to empower researchers to focus on the degree of contextualization and generalizability that is appropriate for the type of knowledge or theory they want to develop. Nevertheless, it should be emphasized that researchers must give explicit consideration to their research design, the details of the context in which the research will be conducted, and the contexts for which the findings may reasonably be relevant and useful.

10.2 Ethical Considerations

Ethical considerations are always relevant and mandatory for any human-factors IT-related research (as well as any research with human subjects in general; Belmont Report, 1979). The Norwegian National Committees for Research Ethics provide four general principles for conducting research[1]: respect (participants shall be treated with respect), good consequences (researchers shall seek to ensure that their activities produce good consequences and that any adverse consequences are within the limits of acceptability), fairness (research projects shall be designed and implemented fairly), and integrity (researchers shall comply with recognized norms and behave responsibly, openly, and honestly toward their colleagues and the public). For experimental studies, these principles are of paramount importance, since researchers may willfully manipulate the independent variable with the goal of observing a change (Shadish et al. 2002). As per the European Commission's report on Ethics for Researchers (European Commission, 2013), three main hallmarks of ethical research underpin the notion of "informed consent": adequate information (being provided with all the necessary information), voluntariness (agreeing voluntarily to take part), and competence (being capable of grasping fully the potential risks of participation).

Ethical and methodological considerations are central when designing an experiment. For example, measures used to increase validity (e.g., deception of participants by using cover stories to orient them away from understanding the RQs) have been criticized (große Deters et al., 2019), as have approaches that seek to increase ecological validity by waiving informed consent (Grimmelmann, 2015). Nevertheless, there is a consensus that explaining and debriefing participants after the experiment is mandatory in all cases (Belmont Report, 1979). Today, the involvement of and approval from an independent ethics committee is mandatory before conducting experimental research. Different countries employ different approaches on how to form and include ethics committees. For instance, some countries have Institutional Review Boards (IRBs), whereas others have national review boards. Nevertheless, today there are established institutional, national, and international regulations, such as the EU's General Data Protection Regulations (GDPR; https://gdpr.eu/), which provide guidelines for human-factors research such as in the fields of learning technology and CCI.

In the context of digital learning and learner-generated data, we have seen a number of endeavors and tools during the last decade. For instance, Slade and Prinsloo (2013) introduced a framework with a focus on ethics in digital learning and learning analytics. Other notable contributions are the JISC code of practice[2] and the DELICATE framework (see Drachsler & Greller, 2016), which are useful tools to support learning technology research and practice. More recently, the International Council for Open and Distant Education (ICDE) produced a set of

---

[1] https://www.forskningsetikk.no/en/guidelines/general-guidelines/
[2] https://www.jisc.ac.uk/guides/code-of-practice-for-learning-analytics

guidelines for ethically informed practice that is expected to guide research in digital learning and learning analytics across the world (Slade & Tait, 2019). In summary, the main ethical considerations in relation to learner-generated data can be grouped into the following categories.

Privacy considerations: how personal data is being observed and protected from unauthorized use. Practices of un-linking linked data, anonymization, and codification are often used (when possible).

Data ownership considerations: information about the ownership, use, and distribution of data. This is another important consideration that protects participants' rights, for example, by ensuring that data will not be passed on or used for unintended additional purposes.

Consent considerations: mandatory provision of documentation that clearly describes the processes involved in data collection and analysis. Consent must be received from each individual participant (or, in the case of children, assent from the individual and consent from the legal guardian) before any experimental study.

Transparency considerations: providing the necessary information and being transparent with respect to which data will be collected, why and how they are going to be analyzed, and under what conditions.

Although this point has already been mentioned, it is important to emphasize that some categories of participants require special attention.

Children. This is the most relevant category for this chapter, since it is central to CCI as well as to learning technology (e.g., in K-12 education). The European Commission's report on Ethics for Researchers (European Commission, 2013) clarifies that when children are involved in research, care and consideration are pivotal. In addition, it requires a clear justification for involving children in research ("the involvement of children in the research must be absolutely necessary and, if so, all particular ethical sensitivities that relate to research involving children must be identified and taken into account") and provides a detailed section on the use of children in research in the European Textbook on Ethics in Research (European Commission, 2010, pp. 65–74).

Vulnerable adults. This category includes, but is not limited to, elderly people, people with learning difficulties, and severely injured patients.

People from certain cultural or traditional backgrounds. In some communities, notions of individuality, written permission, or written agreement do not exist, and certain groups (such as women) may not be permitted to act autonomously. In such communities, the European Commission (2013) clarifies that "strategies must be developed to address these issues with respect for the specificities of the situation."

In addition to these categories that clearly require special attention, it is important for the researcher to consider any potential unequal power relationships (Levine et al., 2004). For example, students, teachers, and children might find themselves in a situation where they experience discomfort (e.g., having to act in certain ways in

10.2 Ethical Considerations

front of their teachers or parents) or even disadvantages (e.g., being socially excluded if they decide not to participate in the study). This puts the voluntariness of their participation in question, and researchers should take all appropriate measures to avoid potential negative effects of participation, emotional stress, or other discomfort (große Deters et al., 2019).

In recent years, we have seen extensive discussion on ethical challenges in the design and use of interactive technologies for children (Hourcade et al., 2017). We have also seen a slight shift in publication venues with respect to ethical considerations in human-factors IT-related research. For example, most publication venues do not require an ethical statement from the authors, which means that ethical issues experienced during the studies may not have been properly reported. However, some publication venues, such as the IDC and *IJCCI*,[3] now require a dedicated section (called, for example, "Selection and participation") in which the authors of the paper describe how the participants were selected, what assent/consent processes were used (i.e., what the participants were told), how the participants were treated, how data sharing was communicated, and any additional ethical considerations. Although the introduction of such a mandatory section in research papers (as with any other regulation-driven checkbox exercise) cannot enforce in-depth consideration of the potential ethical challenges that might emerge from experimentation, it definitely helps by providing a baseline and a certain level of awareness in research communities.

Before closing this subsection, it is important to note that important issues such as children's privacy, AI, social media, and media sharing have not been extensively covered in this book, owing to limitations of space and scope. However, we would like to bring out some of these issues in this final paragraph. Today's children are growing up with technologies that use sensor data and data-driven interactions (e.g., multitouch technology and motion-based technology). Their dispositions over the use of their personal data (e.g., voice interfaces and other affordances that rely on biometric recognition) might be different from those of adults. Therefore, these technological advancements pose fundamental questions as to which technological futures we should be developing and how we face and mediate ethical issues and dilemmas when doing research or designing technology to support children's learning, play, and living (Antle et al., 2021; Eriksson et al., 2021). Contemporary technologies are often "invisible" (e.g., ubiquitous systems), and their intelligence is fueled by unconsciously produced data and sophisticated AI techniques that evolve continually and are in daily use. Future work should consider the ethical issues and dilemmas that emerge from this, and we must proceed with care and responsibility around the potential implications of our research designs, methods and practices, and the resulting technologies.

---

[3] https://www.elsevier.com/journals/international-journal-of-child-computer-interaction/2212-8689/guide-for-authors

10.3 Working with Children

Researchers conducting experimental studies with children might be required to employ different methods, approaches and techniques, as observed in much of the CCI research literature and a recent dedicated chapter (Markopoulos et al., 2021). Nevertheless, we would like to offer a summary of the motivations for and importance of employing child-centered approaches that focus on individual abilities. One example is the use of a traditional verbal questionnaire; such an instrument assumes that respondents are able to think abstractly about their experience. However, children younger than 12 (i.e., those in middle childhood, or at the stage of concrete operations in the Piagetian tradition) have not yet developed these skills; instead, their thinking processes are based on mental representations that relate to concrete events, objects, or experiences. This must be taken into account when adapting the measurement method to the level of cognitive development of the child participant. Following this line of reasoning and related work in child development and psychology (Harter & Pike, 1984), most CCI research methods (e.g., smileyometers and fun sorters; Read & MacFarlane, 2006; see also Fig. 10.1) use visual methods (or observations and qualitative, checklist-based measurements), which we know are more effective than verbal methods (Döring et al., 2010). Such visual analogs represent specific situations, behaviors, and people to whom the child can easily relate.

Besides the actual instruments used, it is important for CCI and learning technology researchers to consider potential collusion (e.g., when administering questionnaires to a group of children in one place). When it comes to open-ended questions and embodied communication, it is likely that the researcher will be unable to work out what all the words and body signals mean. Moreover, some children will choose

Fig. 10.1 Top: The Smileyometer, a Likert-style visual analog scale (VAS) that was designed with the help of children. Bottom: A completed fun sorter, which allows children to rank items against one or more constructs. (From Read & MacFarlane, 2006; with permission by ACM)

to skip some tasks, not follow the depicted usage scenario, or not answer all the questions. This often happens in CCI research, and it is important for the researcher to be able to orchestrate the experiment in real time while considering potential reasons and interpreting the results accordingly. Potential complications can be that the children are tired or bored, they cannot read or understand the question, they do not know the answer or how to write it, or any combination of these reasons (Markopoulos et al., 2021). In recent years, we have seen a plethora of tools used to collect children's opinions and experiences (e.g., the Fun toolkit and laddering). There are also different ways to adapt or modify an instrument from research with adults so that it can support CCI research with children as participants.

References

Antle, N. A., Frauenberger, F., Landoni, M., & Fails, J. A. (2021). Ethics in CCI [special issue]. *International Journal of Child-Computer Interaction, 32*, 100386.
Belmont Report. (1979). *Ethical principles and guidelines for the protection of human subjects of research*. National Commission for the Protection of Human Subjects of Biomedical and Behavioral Research, U.S. Department of Health & Human Services.
Cheng, Z., Dimoka, A., & Pavlou, P. A. (2016). Context may be king, but generalizability is the emperor! *Journal of Information Technology, 31*(3), 257–264.
Davison, R. M., & Martinsons, M. G. (2016). Context is king! Considering particularism in research design and reporting. *Journal of Information Technology, 31*(3), 241–249.
Deaton, A. (2010). Instruments, randomization, and learning about development. *Journal of Economic Literature, 48*, 424–455.
Döring, A. K., Blauensteiner, A., Aryus, K., Drögekamp, L., & Bilsky, W. (2010). Assessing values at an early age: The picture-based value survey for children. *Journal of Personality Assessment, 92*, 439–448. https://doi.org/10.1080/00223891.2010.497423
Drachsler, H., & Greller, W. (2016). Privacy and analytics: It's a DELICATE issue a checklist for trusted learning analytics. In *Proceedings of the sixth international conference on learning analytics & knowledge* (pp. 89–98).
Eriksson, E., Barendregt, W., & Torgersson, O. (2021). Ethical dilemmas experienced by students in child-computer interaction – A case study. *International Journal of Child-Computer Interaction, 100341*.
European Commission. (2013). *Ethics for researchers. Facilitating research excellence in FP17*. Retrieved June 2, 2021, from http://ec.europa.eu/research/participants/data/ref/fp7/89888/ethics-for-researchers_en.pdf.
European Commission. Directorate General for Research. (2010). *European textbook of ethics in research*. European Commission. Retrieved June 2, 2021, from https://op.europa.eu/en/publication-detail/-/publication/0f37f142-c333-40a8-90a7-bba25c314720/language-en
Ferguson, R., Clow, D., Macfadyen, L., Essa, A., Dawson, S., & Alexander, S. (2014). Setting learning analytics in context: Overcoming the barriers to large-scale adoption. In *Proceedings of the 4th international conference on learning analytics and knowledge* (pp. 251–253).
Grimmelmann, J. (2015). The law and ethics of experiments on social media users. *Colorado Technology Law Journal, 13*, 219.
große Deters, F., Tams, S., Johnston, A., & Thatcher, J. (2019). Designing experimental studies. In *ICIS 2019*. https://aisel.aisnet.org/icis2019/pdws/pdws/8
Harter, S., & Pike, R. (1984). The pictorial scale of perceived competence and social acceptance for young children. *Child Development, 55*, 1969–1982. https://doi.org/10.2307/1129772
Höök, K., & Löwgren, J. (2012). Strong concepts: Intermediate-level knowledge in interaction design research. *ACM Transactions on Computer-Human Interaction (TOCHI), 19*(3), 1–18.

Höök, K., Dalsgaard, P., Reeves, S., Bardzell, J., Löwgren, J., Stolterman, E., & Rogers, Y. (2015). Knowledge production in interaction design. In *Proceedings of the 33rd annual ACM conference extended abstracts on human factors in computing systems* (pp. 2429–2432).

Hourcade, J. P., Zeising, A., Iversen, O. S., Pares, N., Eisenberg, M., Quintana, C., & Skov, M. B. (2017). Child-computer interaction sig: Ethics and values. In *Proceedings of the 2017 CHI conference extended abstracts on human factors in computing systems* (pp. 1334–1337).

Lee, A. S., & Baskerville, R. L. (2012). Conceptualizing generalizability: New contributions and a reply. *MIS Quarterly, 36*(3), 749–761.

Levine, C., Faden, R., Grady, C., Hammerschmidt, D., Eckenwiler, L., & Sugarman, J. (2004). The limitations of "vulnerability" as a protection for human research participants. *The American Journal of Bioethics, 4*(3), 44–49.

Markopoulos, P., Read, J. C., & Giannakos, M. (2021). Design of digital technologies for children. *Handbook of human factors and ergonomics*, 1287–1304.

Polit, D. F., & Beck, C. T. (2010). Generalization in quantitative and qualitative research: Myths and strategies. *International Journal of Nursing Studies, 47*(11), 1451–1458.

Read, J. C., & MacFarlane, S. (2006). Using the fun toolkit and other survey methods to gather opinions in child computer interaction. In *Proceedings of the 2006 conference on Interaction design and children* (pp. 81–88).

Sao Pedro, M. A., Baker, R. S., & Gobert, J. D. (2013). What different kinds of stratification can reveal about the generalizability of data-mined skill assessment models. In *Proceedings of the 3rd international conference on learning analytics and knowledge* (pp. 190–194).

Seddon, P., & Scheepers, R. (2012). Towards the improved treatment of generalization of knowledge claims in IS research: Drawing general conclusions from samples. *European Journal of Information Systems, 21*(1), 6–21.

Shadish, W. R., Cook, T. D., & Campbell, D. T. (2002). *Experimental and quasi-experimental designs for generalized causal inference*. Houghton Mifflin.

Sharma, K., Niforatos, E., Giannakos, M., & Kostakos, E. (2020). Assessing cognitive performance using physiological and facial features: Generalizing across contexts. *Proceedings of the ACM on Interactive, Mobile, Wearable and Ubiquitous Technologies, 4*, 1–41.

Sharma, K., & Giannakos, M. (2020). Multimodal data capabilities for learning: What can multimodal data tell us about learning?. *British Journal of Educational Technology, 51*(5), 1450–1484.

Siemens, G., & Baker, RSD (2012). Learning analytics and educational data mining: Towards communication and collaboration. In *Proceedings of the 2nd international conference on learning analytics and knowledge* (pp. 252–254).

Slade, S., & Prinsloo, P. (2013). Learning analytics: Ethical issues and dilemmas. *American Behavioral Scientist, 57*(10), 1510–1529.

Slade, S., & Tait, A. (2019). *Global guidelines: Ethics in learning analytics*. https://www.icde.org/icde-news/new-report-on-ethics-in-learning-analytics

Open Access This chapter is licensed under the terms of the Creative Commons Attribution 4.0 International License (http://creativecommons.org/licenses/by/4.0/), which permits use, sharing, adaptation, distribution and reproduction in any medium or format, as long as you give appropriate credit to the original author(s) and the source, provide a link to the Creative Commons license and indicate if changes were made.

The images or other third party material in this chapter are included in the chapter's Creative Commons license, unless indicated otherwise in a credit line to the material. If material is not included in the chapter's Creative Commons license and your intended use is not permitted by statutory regulation or exceeds the permitted use, you will need to obtain permission directly from the copyright holder.

Chapter 11
Summary and Reflections for Learning Technology and CCI Research

Abstract In this chapter we present a summary of the book, and discuss how the book can support learning technology and CCI researchers. Moreover, we provide some concluding remarks and thoughts for the future of learning technology and CCI research.

Keywords Learning technology · Child-computer interaction · Summary · Experiments

In this book, we have introduced and discussed ways in which experiments and the associated methods and techniques can be employed in the context of learning technology and CCI. The main aim is to clarify the various methods and techniques needed by a researcher to be able to design and conduct a research study efficiently. Understanding of the various methodological decisions will ensure that a learning technology and/or CCI researcher will be able to make optimal decisions that promote high internal validity, make it possible to attribute findings to treatment variations, and identify potential confounding or extraneous factors.

We have also elaborated on the reasons for focusing on both learning technology and CCI and why we put them together. Given the inherent connections between the learning technology and CCI fields and UIs (how children/learners interact with a technology) and the respective research designs (e.g., in most cases we are introducing a new technological innovation to the experimental groups), we have provided fundamental knowledge on the design of educational interfaces and visualizations, with a focus on learning dashboards. In preparation for our discussion of the common forms of experimentation, we also considered the role of the artefact in contemporary learning technology and CCI research, and we set out the fundamentals of treatment design and artefact-centered evaluations.

We then presented different research designs: between-subjects, within-subjects, and mixed research designs. We set out common decision factors when considering the use of between- and within- subjects designs, using examples from the CCI and learning technology research fields. We discussed four common types of experimentation and their qualities: randomized (or true) experiment, quasi-experiment, repeated measures, and time series experiment. We also discussed the importance of internal validity and identified typical threats to that validity, such as unequal treatments and confounding or extraneous factors.

Next, we provided fundamental guidance on how a learning technology/CCI researcher can identify the most appropriate data analysis approach for their study. Given the importance of disseminating research results and publishing them in high-quality venues, we also focused on writing quality, standards, and style conventions. We explained how to organize a typical article/report in the field, identifying the six important high-level sections (introduction, background and related work, methods, findings, discussion, and conclusion and further research), common criteria used by reviewers, pitfalls in learning technology/CCI research, and some useful practices for junior researchers.

Given contemporary advances in data science, AI and sensor data, and their impact on both learning technology and CCI research, we gave a brief overview of how those developments have affected learning technology and CCI research, suggesting potential worthwhile uses. In addition, we briefly discussed three important issues that a learning technology and CCI researcher needs to be aware of: the importance of the context, ethical considerations, and working with children. There is a growing literature on each of these areas (e.g., Shibani et al., 2019; Van Mechelen et al., 2020; Romero & Ventura, 2017; Luckin & Cukurova, 2019), and we by no means claim to have covered them in detail; nevertheless, this book would have been incomplete if we had not provided an introduction to these important issues.

Although this book does not focus exclusively on experimentation, it is a topic that has received much attention. The use of experimentation has been criticized (e.g., see Ross & Morrison, 2013) as force-fitting, as fixated on internal validity, or even as being in conflict with potential improvements in the use of technology for supporting learning, play, and our lives generally. However, we want to emphasize in this closing chapter that the purpose of this book is not to promote or criticize the experimental method, but rather to provide direction for its effective use in learning technology and CCI research. Like any other research method, experimental methods can be employed "badly", and it is important for a learning technology/CCI researcher to be able to apply experimental methods in a way that aligns with the RQs and that takes into account the contextual particularities. Moreover, to improve sensemaking, experiments can (and in many cases should) be used in conjunction with other research methods and approaches.

As we close this book, we hope that learning technology and CCI researchers can benefit from it, and we emphasize the role that researchers play as research designers who employ, adapt, alter, and expand research methods to accommodate contextual complexion, relevant theories, and the scientific inquiry of focus. The ultimate goal is to increase understanding of how technological affordances and technology-mediated practices can enhance our capabilities (e.g., as learners and children) and support the mental processes involved in gaining knowledge and comprehension.

References

Luckin, R., & Cukurova, M. (2019). Designing educational technologies in the age of AI: A learning sciences-driven approach. *British Journal of Educational Technology, 50*(6), 2824–2838.

Romero, C., & Ventura, S. (2017). Educational data science in massive open online courses. *Wiley Interdisciplinary Reviews: Data Mining and Knowledge Discovery, 7*(1), e1187.

Ross, S. M., & Morrison, G. R. (2013). Experimental research methods. In *Handbook of research on educational communications and technology* (pp. 1007–1029). Routledge.

Shibani, A., Knight, S., & Shum, S. B. (2019). Contextualizable learning analytics design: A generic model and writing analytics evaluations. In *Proceedings of the 9th international conference on learning analytics & knowledge* (pp. 210–219).

Van Mechelen, M., Baykal, G. E., Dindler, C., Eriksson, E., & Iversen, O. S. (2020). 18 Years of ethics in child-computer interaction research: A systematic literature review. In *Proceedings of the interaction design and children conference* (pp. 161–183).

Open Access This chapter is licensed under the terms of the Creative Commons Attribution 4.0 International License (http://creativecommons.org/licenses/by/4.0/), which permits use, sharing, adaptation, distribution and reproduction in any medium or format, as long as you give appropriate credit to the original author(s) and the source, provide a link to the Creative Commons license and indicate if changes were made.

The images or other third party material in this chapter are included in the chapter's Creative Commons license, unless indicated otherwise in a credit line to the material. If material is not included in the chapter's Creative Commons license and your intended use is not permitted by statutory regulation or exceeds the permitted use, you will need to obtain permission directly from the copyright holder.

The manufacturer's authorised representative in the EU is Springer Nature Customer Service Centre GmbH, Europaplatz 3, 69115 Heidelberg, Germany. If you have any concerns regarding our products, please contact ProductSafety@springernature.com

Printed and bound by CPI Group (UK) Ltd, Croydon, CR0 4YY
23/03/2026
02076446-0013